*Grapes
from Thorns*

Dean Acheson died on October 12, 1971. On the next day, in the Senate of the United States, Senator Walter Mondale delivered the following tribute:

Mr. President, there will be many tributes to Dean Acheson.

There are so many in his debt—the nations of Western Europe, whose vitality and freedom are so largely the legacy of his devotion to the Atlantic Alliance, and of course the people of the United States, to whom he gave gifts of public service unmatched in our memory.

But the greatness of Dean Acheson was more than his historic defense of the Western community, and more than the gift of his enormous talent to the governing of his country.

His greatness ran to those rare depths of the man himself. He also showed us grace and total self-respect and a brave, unyielding loyalty to friends and ideals under fire. How we will miss his brilliance and dedication, but I wonder if we will not miss even more these personal strengths of character which made him an extraordinary human being as well as a singular public servant.

And if we lose—as I fear we are losing now—this inner integrity in public life, neither ability nor passion will be enough to rescue us.

Perhaps that is the ultimate counsel from a man who so often steered us safe from the base and the dangerous.

He said it with characteristic eloquence to a Senate Committee in 1950.

> One must be true to the things by which one lives. The counsels of discretion and cowardice are appealing. The

safe course is to avoid situations which are disagreeable and dangerous. Such a course might get one by the issue of the moment, but it has bitter and evil consequences. In the long days and years which stretch beyond that moment of decision, one must live with one's self; and the consequences of living with a decision which one knows has sprung from timidity and cowardice go to the roots of one's life. It is not merely a question of peace of mind, although that is vital; it is a matter of integrity of character.

Books by Dean Acheson

A Democrat Looks at His Party
A Citizen Looks at Congress
Power and Diplomacy
Sketches from Life
Morning and Noon
Present at the Creation
Fragments of My Fleece
Grapes from Thorns

DEAN ACHESON

Grapes
from Thorns

⋘

W · W · NORTON & COMPANY · INC

NEW YORK

Library of Congress Cataloging in Publication Data

Acheson, Dean Gooderham, 1893–1971.
    Grapes from thorns. NEW YORK, NORTON, 1972

253p.

    I. Title.
    E748.A15A293   081   76–39604
    ISBN 0–393–05254–0

E748
A15
A293

Published simultaneously in Canada
by George J. McLeod Limited, Toronto

The Holiday and *The Earrings,* Copyright © 1966. The Atlantic Monthly
Company, Boston, Mass.; *The Fairy Princess,* Copyright © 1965 by The
Reporter Magazine Company; *Range Practice* © Copyright 1968 by Ameri-
can Heritage Publishing Co., Inc. Reprinted by permission from American
Heritage Magazine, February 1968; *Voice of Experience* and *William
Duncan Herridge* from The Washington Post; *The Test of Happiness,
Thoughts about Thought in High Places, The American Image Will Take
Care of Itself,* and *Hume Wrong* © 1958/59/65/54 by The New York
Times Company. Reprinted by permission; *Morality, Moralism, and Diplomacy* from the Yale Review, copyright Yale University Press; *The Illusion of Disengagement* from Foreign Affairs; *Canada: "Stern Daughter of
the Voice of God,"* from *Neighbors Taken for Granted,* © Praeger Pub-
lishers, Inc.; *The Supreme Artist* © The Observer, London; *Ernest Bevin*
from BBC Broadcast, 1957.

To Jane, David, and Mary

Contents

Contents

Contents

13

Preface

My secretary of many years, Miss Barbara Evans, and I have been going through our records with a view to melting most of them down to the unblemished paper from which they sprang. In the course of doing so, we discovered an unexpected answer to a question asked two millennia ago: "Do men gather grapes of thorns or figs of thistles?" We found that occasionally they did and that *we* did. Here and there among the thorns of the law and the thistles of politics and diplomacy we found some fruit that had retained its flavor and, in some cases, its tartness. These finds are presented as we found them without the polishing of second thought. A few thorns that had become embedded in the fruit have been removed.

Part One ⫷

Stories

The Holiday

Holidays were all too rare for State Department people during the war years. This describes an extemporized attempt to take a day off.

Secretary of State Cordell Hull was not one to "pay much mind," as he would put it, to his minions. With a few he feuded; to a few he listened—rather more, the outsiders thought, than their contributions warranted; but for the most part, he let the rest of us go our own way, which often led nowhere in particular. So, when I was shown into his office in the old State, War, and Navy Building after three weeks' absence presiding over an international conference, it would not have surprised me if he had not noticed that I had been away.

The Atlantic Monthly, October, 1966.

19

Stories

His greeting disclosed nothing. When he was displeased, his greeting was, "Come in, Doctor." I never thought that this reflected a prejudice against the medical profession, perhaps not even against doctors of philosophy, but vaguely against know-it-alls. Normally, he merely looked over his black-rimmed pince-nez, held to him by its black ribbon, and asked, "How you feelin'?" I made the conventional claim to good health. The Secretary took off his pince-nez and gave me a searching look. "You're kinda peaked-lookin'," he observed.

If I wasn't, I should have been. For three exhausting weeks the conference had maneuvered around proposals for post-war relief. UNRRA was in gestation. FDR's newfound enthusiasm for international organization, born of his coining a year before that delusive phrase "the United Nations," was to bring together through an international agency the supplicants for and the givers of relief. The problems involved were not complicated, but difficult of solution, since the idea that it was more blessed—or at any rate more desirable —to give than to receive was not the postulate of the conference. My job was to be the John the Baptist of the Marshall Plan, without giving the receivers of relief an unrestricted drawing account on the United States Treasury.

This is not the story of that conference. It is enough to say that for some reason, not altogether clear to me after the lapse of twenty-three years, it seemed to require innumerable midnight conferences and the consumption of considerable quantities of what the revenue laws call vinous and spiritous liquors. I remember

The Holiday

being alarmed at the condition of one colleague whose eyes seemed to be disappearing behind narrowing slits. Others urged me not to worry since if worst came to worst, we could always buy him a seeing-eye dog. I remember, too, the staunch support of a delightful Cuban, representing the now much abused Batista regime, who upbraided his fellow Latinos, saying that they reminded him of the crowds on the day of a great fiesta, marching into the cathedral carrying banners and singing a Te Deum, but when the offering plate was passed, slipping out a side door.

At any rate, I was tired and admitted it. The Secretary nodded with his air of infinite benevolence. "Better take a holiday," he said.

It couldn't be true. No one took a holiday. "Don't you know there's a war on?" was the vicious quasher of ideas like that.

"But, Mr. Secretary," I gasped.

Cordell Hull was a man of decision. He had had enough of this interruption and report. "Yes," he said, with an air of finality and dismissal, "take the afternoon off." He put on his pince-nez and picked up a paper; I gathered my unmentioned report and left.

A few minutes later on the telephone: "Listen carefully, my dear," I said. "Whatever you have planned for lunch and the afternoon is off. As soon as I can get home, we leave on a holiday, at the Secretary's command. You may not have noticed it, but his more compassionate eye sees me badly in need of a rest."

"But where are we going? How? What do I pack?"

"That is secret," I cut in. "Even the longest holiday

can be unraveled by a woman's tongue. The immediate thing is to have the bicycles brought up from the cellar and dusted. When I get home we can see to the tires." I hung up while I had the advantage of mystery. The plan was forming as I got an official car, unavailable by law for personal use, to drive me home before my seniors got it for the governmental purpose of taking them to lunch.

The bicycles were ready, and the lady's curiosity had overcome annoyance by the time we were wheeling them to the filling station for air and a few drops of oil. Then, using the momentum of the steep plunge from P Street down to Rock Creek and Potomac Parkway, we skimmed along in glorious December sunshine. The creek soon gave way to the majestic river in "raiment white and glistering," in the Prayer Book's phrase. Patient fishermen dozed along the embankment. Gulls circled and screamed around a towboat taking a string of empty barges downstream to Newport News. An eight-oared shell from Georgetown University paddled slowly up, its blades flashing in rhythm with the coxswain's chant, the crew absorbing wisdom from the coach's megaphone. The sight always takes me back nostalgically to afternoon paddles in New Haven harbor when the wind had dropped, to the ecstasy of the long reach of a crew in perfect balance and rhythm, to the breathtaking stab of icy water as a wavelet struck a forward outrigger. On we went, past Mrs. Whitney's sculptured memorial to the *Titanic* dead, skirting the Lincoln Memorial by the passage under the bridge, and cutting off to the left toward the Tidal Basin, passing the small village of "temporary" buildings which housed government offices in their hot ugliness for twenty years. The basin, now deserted and its cherry trees bare, reflected the calm, cold beauty of the Jefferson Memorial.

We were now on the last lap. A dive under Fourteenth Street and the railroad tracks, a short pedal along Maine Avenue, and we reached Fisherman's Wharf. Twenty-five years ago a row of oyster and clam bars (known as "raw bars"), seafood restaurants, and fish markets stretched along the waterfront. Today the flow of a Vesuvius of concrete has covered them all to create a mad swirl of overpasses, underpasses, and bridges, to the utter confusion of the motorist without an inertial guidance system.

Our destination was called Eacho Fish. Rumor had it that Eacho was the name of the proprietor, who dispensed seafood, beer, and spirits. But another school asserted that it was a command in the vernacular to "eat your fish." Be that as it may, the oysters and clams were fresh and salty from Chesapeake Bay, and the fish and crabs only a few hours from water to pan. A cocktail or two carried us through waiting while the barman opened oysters and clams until we had to call a halt. Then we moved on to butterfish so fresh, fat, and sweet as to be food for Valhalla.

So intent were we on the nourishment of the inner man and woman that a party at the other end of the long bar quite escaped notice until its growing noisiness and evident interest in us drew our attention. The director of the discussion was a plump woman well past the first, and perhaps the second, blush of youth and responding generously to the inspiration of Mr. Eacho's cocktails. Her friends were trying to modify her enthusiasm. We thought we could best help them by good-natured aloofness. So we smiled at her sallies and occasionally waved. In this we were wrong. She announced loudly, "Well, I'm going to find out!" and made her way, a bit unsteadily, along the bar in our direction.

As she reached us, I made a half-hearted gesture of rising, motioned to the adjoining stool, and murmured, "Won't you sit down?"

She did, with something of a flop. Then, peering at me with unfocused intensity, she asserted more than asked, "You're Robert Montgomery, aren't you?"

While it seems impossible, it is doubtless true that since that December day generations have grown up in the land who know the Beatles but have never heard of Robert Montgomery. For them I explain that he was a motion-picture actor for whom any right-thinking man would have been honored to have been taken —far more so than for any or all of the Beatles. In view of the circumstances, including the fact that I must clearly know the answer to her question, the wiser course seemed to be neither to affirm nor deny.

"Why be so formal?" I asked. "Why not just call me Bob?"

With that she made a lunge and planted a moist kiss in the neighborhood of an ear. When we managed to get disentangled, she shouted down the bar, "I'm right." Then turning back to us with a smirk, she pressed on: "And is this Mrs. Montgomery?"

A glance at my companion suggested the need for caution. "Not yet," I murmured.

"This calls for a drink," she announced, and started back toward her friends.

"Robert," said my companion, "I'm leaving."

With a brief pause by the cash register, I followed amid cheers, and with some vigorous pedaling caught up.

"Why be so formal?" I repeated my question, but drew no smile.

Instead, "You didn't ask *me* to call you Bob," she said, and pushed on.

The sun was slanting down to the southwest, warning that the flood of homebound traffic would soon engulf us. We sped along in silence and beat it to the stiff walk uphill to P Street. Two blocks more, and we were wheeling in our back gate as the sun disappeared. The lady was chuckling.

"One thing I will say for you," she offered. "When you plan a holiday, there's not a dull moment in it."

The Fairy Princess

The Grand Chamberlain and the Court attendants brought the Guest into the Queen's reception room, like a duck guiding a cygnet which had been caught up among the ducklings. After much fluttering, muttering, and busying about, the servants were left, grouped together at the far end of the audience chamber; and the Guest and the Royal Interpreter were led to the raised gold-upholstered sofa, the contribution of a Gallic decorator to the conception of Asian splendor, where the Queen sat, solid, genial, and gray, fanning herself. It was very warm. The Guest bowed, palms pressed together before his chest as in prayer. The Queen inclined her head. Greetings and gifts were exchanged. The Grand Chamberlain, fussing, withdrew out of hearing. The Queen, the Guest, and the Royal Interpreter were alone.

The Reporter, October 7, 1965.

"How did you come?" asked the Queen. "By the new planes?"

"No," said the Guest, "by the old road—but it's no longer that. By the great new road the Americans have made where the old road was, changing everything."

"Not as much as you think," said the Queen. "Did you see the villagers coming to town now that the dry season is here and the river is low?"

"An endless procession," answered the Guest. "Village after village along the shoulder of the highway; miniature oxcarts, miniature oxen, miniature people, miniature dogs—the original essence of dog, father of all breeds of dog—plodding along, cart after cart, trucks and busses roaring past in both directions. The people seem the same; but can they be?"

"Why not? Did you expect them to be taking vitamins made by a Belgian syndicate with their rice? For a thousand years—who knows how many thousand years—the Great River has drawn back and opened its riches to us, tons and tons of fish scooped out of it to give protein and vitamin. Can a highway change that?"

"As you yourself said, Majesty, 'Why not?'" the Guest replied. "Highways, planes, radio, newspapers! Ideas come by them. People look the same. Perhaps act the same. But are they the same? How do you know? You see them from the top; how do they look from the bottom?"

"How does a flower look from the bottom?" asked the Queen. "A tangle of roots and earthworms. I prefer the view from above; but I can see that it is a matter of taste and one's nature."

Stories

She stopped, as though reaching beyond the edge of memory, and then went on. "Long ago, when I was a young Princess, I was being driven along this same way in my carriage. Of course it was the old road, before the Americans came. But it was the same time of year, the dry season, and the villagers were coming to the city for fish oil, as you saw them today. Oxcart after oxcart, mile after mile of them; the road was crowded, dusty, and pulsing with life.

"It was late afternoon, and already families were drawing off the road for the night, unyoking the oxen, getting the evening meal, putting the smaller children to bed in the cart. Then we came to a block. Something ahead had stopped traffic. No use to turn, even if we could; for we were soon blocked behind too. So we pushed along, the servants shouting to make way for the Princess. Pretty soon we heard wailing ahead, and soon after came on the reason.

"An ox lay dead beside the road, one of a peasant's span. The entire village had stopped to lament. The tragedy was real enough. To buy another ox would have taken all that had been saved in the year for fish oil. Yet without another ox the family could neither go on nor go back. For the moment the narcotic of lament deadened the dilemma.

" 'Find out for me,' I asked a servant, 'the price of an ox.'

" 'About a hundred piastres, Highness, give or take a bit depending on the ox,' he reported.

"Looking in my purse, I found just one hundred piastres, no more, no less. Giving them to the servant,

I bade him be off to buy an ox. Soon he came back with one, and I sent him with it, as a gift from the King, to the bereaved peasant."

The Queen paused, leaning forward in the intensity of her telling. "In the briefest moment," she went on, "in the twinkling of an eye, all was changed. The wailing stopped. A rising murmur rustled through the people like a freshening breeze through trees. Then cheering, shouts, laughter, and a rush toward my carriage. People kissed my ring, the carriage, the horses. They danced about us. They sang. Where there had been sorrow, now was only joy, gaiety, and laughter."

The Queen stopped, but the Guest knew that she had not finished. "Friend," she began again, "you said that I see people only from above and ask how I know what changes them. I might make an answer, but I should like to know yours. Was it, in my story, only the matter of the ox? A dead ox made them sad; a live ox made them gay? Was it as simple as that?"

"No, Majesty," said the Guest. "It was not that; but it was as simple as that."

"No riddles," cried the Queen. "Out with it."

"It was you yourself," replied the Guest. "For you were a fairy princess, and we all know a fairy princess can change things into their opposites. With one wave of her all-powerful wand, the ugly toad is changed into the most beautiful prince, or the fisherman's hut into a marble palace, or the other way around. It was you that day on the old road who changed people, and—if I may speak with the frankness of an old friend—I wouldn't put it past you now."

Stories

The Queen burst into laughter; she choked and cried with laughter, until the Grand Chamberlain and the servants began to murmur at the other end of the room. When finally she could speak again and met the Guest's perplexed eye, she said, "Look at me. Just look at me! Do I look like a fairy princess?"

It could not be denied that the Queen had made a point, but the Guest was in no position to admit it. With dignity, he adopted a stern tone.

"Majesty," he said, "the test of a fairy princess is not looks but works. You found sorrow; you changed it into joy. That, if I may put it this way, is the spoor of a fairy princess. Furthermore, with respect and deference, this is not a matter for levity. The books are full of reports of most unfortunate exercises of this power by jesting princesses unaware of what in the Pentagon, a sorcerer's castle, is called their capabilities. Believe me, Most Gracious Queen, and do not take it lightly, a Queen may be as likely as not a more mature fairy princess."

The Queen, smiling a gentle and detached smile, was silent for a long moment. Then bestirring herself, she rose and bowed with her hands pressed together.

"Good night, my friend," she said, now quite regal. "You must leave us while we think about our talk." The Guest withdrew.

In the morning the Prince was abstracted and inattentive during the audience he gave the Guest. When the Guest stopped his narrative for want of a listener, the Prince asked him bluntly, "What is all this that

30

you have said to my mother about her being a fairy princess?"

"Highness," said the Guest, "it was only a manner of speaking."

"Manner of speaking indeed," said the Prince. "You have put ideas into her head. God knows what will come of that."

"Your Highness knows better," the Guest protested. "Not put them into her head. They were all there. Only stirred them up and set them circulating."

"Put it any way you like," said the Prince wearily. "She's off again on her passion for changing people. I think she gets it from the Americans. At any rate, it makes me nervous when she talks that way."

"What way, Highness?"

"Well, to begin with, she says that if I do not mind the diet she has prescribed for me, she will turn me from a Prince into an elephant, and ride on me."

"Please, Highness, have no doubt of it. She will. But that, you say, is to begin with. After that, what?"

"Then she wants to change the Americans."

"Into what? Into what?" breathed the Guest.

He thought of the hundreds of Americans he had seen that day—three hundred, four hundred, five hundred—devoted, uncomplicated prophets of progress, planting new crops, building new roads, showing new weapons, upsetting the ancient harmony between the death rate and the birth rate, breaking the repose of untouched minds with Roman letters and Arabic figures, happy in their propagation of the faith. Suddenly he was all but paralyzed by panic, seeing these people as the inhabitants of Johnstown, Pennsylvania, just before the dam burst. How could they be warned? Would they believe a warning?

"Into what?" he asked again. "Into what?"

"That's just it." The Prince embodied exasperation. "I can't get it out of her. She just won't say another word."

The Earrings

Diplomatic dinners in Washington are not the glamorous events which Edwardian novels and memoirs depict them as having been in London. Even thirty years or more ago they were not. Superbly groomed and beautiful women, glittering with jewels, did not provoke equally glittering wit from statesmen toying with the fate of nations. When Washington was much smaller and the diplomatic list less than a third its present length, one could guess who two thirds of the diplomatic guests would be, and time after time one would draw the wife of the same colleague in the little cabinet.

One evening, however, my card informed me that I would take in a partner unknown to me and about whom neither our host's introduction nor cautious inquiries revealed anything. On the way into dinner I

The Atlantic Monthly, January, 1967.

caught a foreign accent, Germanic I guessed, but she rose to none of the flies I cast above her.

Then curiosity had to rest for the moment. Talk at the table had set against us, and her attention was claimed on her other side. My own, though not claimed, was dutifully turned to an only too familiar tale, a colleague's wife. The medical degree she was reputed to have taken must have been in surgery and led on to expertise in probing tender spots. Her aim seemed to be to keep the rest of us in wincing consciousness of inferiority. A friend had told me that when he asked her at one of the diplomatic rumbles who somebody was, she replied, "I'm afraid I can't help you. I know only chiefs of missions." Searching for a safe gambit, I thought I had found one in the absence of her husband. Was he off, I asked, on one of his mysterious missions?

He was not, it turned out, but was, unhappily, under the weather. After expressing insincere solicitude, I carelessly dropped my guard. Was his trouble contagious, and should those of us who had met with him only the day before take prophylactic measures? Surely we needed medical guidance, and who better than she could give it?

"Oh, no," she said, airily, "you have nothing to worry about. You see, this attack of jaundice came from overwork."

It was a neat thrust, lethal but almost painless, and carried off with bland vindictiveness. Deflated, I could only express relief and hope that the sufferer from exhaustion in line of duty might posthumously be

The Earrings

awarded the purple heart. With these pleasantries we
occupied ourselves until the table turned, and I with
it, hopeful of better luck with my unknown partner.

More cautious this time, I waited for her to take the
initiative. After a long look across and down the length
of the table, she leaned conspiratorially toward me.
"Who," she asked, "is that Spanish lady—or is she
South American?—wearing the striking earrings?" We
were soon on target. I knew that our conversation for
the evening was made. Resisting the ancient gag
"That's no lady; that's my wife," I began by whetting
her curiosity.

"Superficially," I said, "the lady is neither Spanish
nor South American, but one of the fairest flowers of
Michigan. I speak with knowledge since I have the
great good fortune of being her husband. And yet how
right you are to think her Spanish and to mention the
earrings!" Right, indeed, since I had bought them myself within the month as a Christmas offering—large
old gold affairs with long pendants dangling bright
semiprecious stones which sparkled as she moved. We
had admired them in the window of Arnold's antique
jewelry shop, long since gone when its home gave way
to the building boom which has transformed down-
town Washington. They had been the success of that
Christmas.

"But you must not stop there!" said the lady. I had
no intention of doing so, only of setting the hook before playing my fish.

The story began, I told her, in the summer of 1588
after the long-running fight from the Lizard through

35

the Channel and up the east coast of England to beyond the Wash. Poor seasick Medina Sidonia with his vast, unwieldy Armada took a fearful beating from the great Drake, who was commanding the Queen's new ships. They had been designed by old John Hawkins. Against much shaking of heads, he had narrowed and lengthened the conventional galleon, doing away with the towering castles on bow and stern so that his ships could sail nearer the wind. He did away, too, with short-range batteries firing man-killing canisters, and substituted broadsides of long-range culverins. He would no longer, he said, fight infantry battles at sea, which Spain must win, but would outsail the Armada, and standing off out of range, batter it to pieces.

Drake did just this. Where he left off, the Lord of Battles took up. He blew the shattered remnant of the Spanish fleet around the north of Scotland and down the west coast of Ireland. The Irish gratefully received wreckage washed ashore. When they found a man, in whom a faint spark of life still lingered, lashed to a spar, they presumed him to be a co-religionist and an enemy of the English, and so treated him kindly. This ragged bit of human flotsam could remember little beyond a confused horror of battle and shipwreck; not even his name. So he was called "Lestrange" and settled down happily where he had been washed ashore.

This touch seemed to me a nice, although faint, connection with truth. My wife's grandmother had been born a Lestrange of County Kerry.

"But the earrings," asked my dinner partner, "where do they come in?"

The Earrings

"He was wearing them! And ever since, contrary to the Salic law, they have descended in the female line. So, you see, with rare perception you grasped the essentials about the dark lady—the suggestion of Spain and the earrings."

My partner continued her rapt gaze down the table. "It sounds just like a novel," she murmured.

I looked at her quickly, but she continued her study. It did, indeed, sound like a novel, because it was one, a best seller by a favorite of the time, Donn Byrne. I would not have dared try the plagiarism on a fellow countrywoman. When the ladies withdrew, an interesting interview would surely occur, but my wife had read *Destiny Bay*, too, and could be counted on to field whatever came her way. It would certainly begin with due warning—something like, "Your husband has been telling me the fascinating tale of your Spanish ancestor and those entrancing earrings."

When we reassembled, I carefully avoided both the connubial eye and my late dinner partner, making innocently for a postprandial companion. My wife did not even look up as she hissed a word at me: "Swine!" It was a small price to pay for escaping a conversation which could have been a bore.

Range Practice

The calendar has it that these events occurred fifty years ago last summer. It is hardly more
credible than that a thousand ages can be like an evening gone. But as President Lincoln said, "we cannot
escape history." Nineteen-sixteen was the year of the
Wilhelmstrasse's amazingly successful plot to distract
President Wilson's attention from the war in Europe
by involving him with Mexico, of General "Black
Jack" Pershing's invasion of Mexico in "hot pursuit"
of Pancho Villa, after that worthy had staged a raid
across the Rio Grande on Columbus, New Mexico.
Poor General Pershing never caught up with Villa.

But President Wilson caught up with the realization
that the United States had no army. Improvising, he
called out the National Guard and mustered it into the
federal service. This is where I came in. Having fin-

American Heritage, February, 1968.

ished the first year of law school and being without plans for the summer, I was easy prey for the press gang in the form of friends in the so-called Yale Battery, Battery D of the Connecticut National Guard's Regiment of Field Artillery. In no time I found myself that lowly form of military life, a private and "driver" in the old horse-drawn field artillery. Garbed in a hilariously ill-fitting uniform and Stetson hat with its red cord, I made my small contribution to the gloriously unorganized confusion of our journey from New Haven to training camp at Tobyhanna in the Pocono hills of Pennsylvania.

None of our batteries had ever owned any horses. Those used in the evening drills in New Haven had been moonlighting, supplementing a more mundane daytime existence as brewery and dray horses. We would get our horses, so we were told, at Tobyhanna. They would come to us from the West—an interesting thought, this. Would we be, we wondered, the first bipeds they had ever seen? Our imagination was far inferior to the reality.

The first disillusion came on arrival. It was with mankind. We had been preceded by a New Jersey regiment which had, quite naturally, appropriated the best sites and everything movable. Our relations with them soon resembled those between colonial contingents in the Continental Army, meaning that had Hessians been handy, we should have preferred them.

Then came the horses. Those assigned to the New Jersey regiment arrived first. Words sink into pallid inadequacy. Our first impressions were gay: a vast pan-

oramic cartoon of our enemy campmates in side-split-
ting trouble. Blithe horse-spirits from the Great Plains
seemed to be enjoying a gymnastic festival, with inani-
mate human forms scattered around them. But the
comedy was not to last.

Our horses emerged from their boxcars strangely
docile. Only occasionally would an eye roll and heels
fly or teeth bare in attempted mayhem or murder. No
more was the landscape gay with mad scenes of separat-
ing centaurs. Over the whole camp a pall settled,
broken only by asthmatic wheezes and horse coughs.
Stable sergeants and veterinary officers hurried about
with worried faces. The wretched horses had caught
cold in the chill night mountain air, so different from
that of their warm, free prairies. The colds had become pneumonia and contagious.

Then they began to die. One has no idea how large
an animal a horse is until faced with the disposal of a
dead one, and in the Poconos, where solid rock lies
barely two feet under the surface! It was no illusion,
to those whose picks drew only sparks, that the bodies
of the deceased grew faster than their graves. Soon we
were all pleading with the sufferers to be of good heart,
not to give up the battle for life; we put slings under
them to keep them on their feet; tenderly gave them
the veterinarians' doses; manned round-the-clock
watches at the stables.

At just this time, far off in the higher echelons of
the Army, some keen leader of men decided to raise
the morale of the troops by inspecting them. The
choice fell on Major General Leonard Wood, late a

physician and Teddy Roosevelt's CO in the Rough
Riders, then commanding the Eastern Department of
the Army and soon to be Governor General of the
Philippines and a presidential aspirant. At that time
not even Alexander the Great would have impressed
us, much less imbued us with martial spirit. We were
sunk too deep in the horse-undertaking business.

A friend was doing midnight-to-four sentry duty at
our stables. Lanterns bobbed and boots slid on stone
as a party approached. Tearing himself away from the
nuances of horse breathing, he shouted "Halt! Who
goes there?" Back came the ominous answer, "The
Commanding General of the Eastern Department."
Rapidly exhausting his knowledge of military repartee,
my friend ordered, "Advance to be recognized." General Wood stepped into the lamplight. The sentry did
not know him from the mayor of Philadelphia, but the
stars on his shoulders were enough, and, anyway, he
had run out of small talk. He managed a snappy salute
and the word "sir!" which seemed safe enough.

General Wood took over. His examination brought
out that the sentry was guarding the battery's stable,
or part of it, and that the stable was, not surprisingly,
inhabited by horses. He then sought to probe the
vaunted initiative of the American soldier. "What
would you do," he asked, "if, while you were on duty,
one of these horses was taken sick?" For a moment the
enormity of this question flooded my friend's mind,
submerging all consciousness of military protocol.
When he could speak, the outrage of it burst through.
"Jesus, General, they're *all* sick!" Like Bret Harte's Ah

Sin, when the ace fell out of his sleeve in the poker game, "subsequent proceedings interested him no more."

At the height of the horse crisis I was ordered to report to the captain's tent. General consensus recognized Captain Carroll Hincks as a good guy. A few years ahead of us at Yale, he had just begun to practice law in New Haven. He did his best to be a good soldier and a good battery commander. To say that his natural gifts lay in his own profession is no disparagement, since he was destined to become a highly respected federal judge, first on the district bench and later on the court of appeals.

The captain began—truth forces me to admit—with a gross understatement, followed by an even grosser untruth. "You may be aware," he said, "of the dissatisfaction of the men with the food being served to them." Remembering the troubles of my friend at the stables, a simple "Yes, sir" seemed an adequate reply. To coin a phrase, the food was God-awful.

"Very well," he went on, "I'm going to give you a great opportunity." A clear lie, obviously. Captains did not give privates opportunities; they only gave them headaches. "You will be promoted to the rank of sergeant and put in charge of the mess."

A nice calculation of the evils before me would have required an advanced type of computer. In the descending circles of hell, horse-burial details were clearly lower than mess sergeants—closer to the central fire and suffering. Mess sergeants suffered only social obloquy. But redemption worked the other way. The horses might get well or all die. But those who became mess sergeants all hope abandoned. Corporals, even little corporals, might become emperors, but no mess sergeant ever got to be a shavetail. However, the captain had not offered me a choice; he had pronounced a judgment. "Yes, sir," I said again, and was dismissed.

As things turned out, life proved tolerable. One help was that the food could not get worse; another, that one of the cooks was not without gifts which, when sober, he could be inspired to use. It only remained to convince the regimental sergeant major that after the cook's Bacchic lapses the true function of the guardhouse was to sober him up, not to reform him. All in all, things began to look up. Although the very nature of the soldier requires that he beef about his food, the beefing in Battery D began to take on almost benevolent profanity. That is, until the major entered our lives.

In real life—if I may put it that way—the major was a professor, a renowned archeologist and explorer of lost civilizations, obvious qualifications for supervising regimental nutrition and hygiene. He turned his attention first to food. The rice we boiled, he correctly pointed out, seemed to flow together, in an unappetizing starchy mass. In the Andes, he said, they prevented this by boiling the rice in paper bags. Aside from the inherent implausibility of this procedure, it seemed to have no relation to the end sought. But the professor-turned-major showed no inclination to debate the point; and an order is an order according to the Articles of War. After all, it seemed to make little difference, since the bags, and even the hemp that tied them, simply disappeared into the gelatinous mass. But our customers found otherwise. They reported an indissoluble residue, impervious to chewing, soon identified as wood pulp. The major was the killing frost that nipped the tender buds of the battery's good will toward me.

Then came the matter of the disposal of the dishwater in which the men washed their mess kits. Neither regulations nor regimental headquarters had considered, much less solved, this problem. However, we in the cookhouse had. We simply tipped the barrel over a small cliff behind the company street. No one criticized this eminently practical solution of a practical problem until the major came along. He regarded it as unhygienic and again found the solution in Andean practice. There they had built fires within horseshoe-shaped, low stone walls and poured dishwater over the hot stones by the dipperful, turning it into a presumably sanitary steam. A ukase was issued to the kitchen police. Sullenly they built the stone horseshoe and, after diligent scrounging for wood, the fire. Appalachian stone proved to be more heat resistant than the Andean variety. An hour's dipping hardly reduced the level of the dishwater and produced no steam. At this point the kitchen police, delivering a succinct statement of their view of the situation in general and of me specifically, poured the whole barrel of water over the fire, and signed off for the night. It was mutiny; but it was magnificent. Next morning, a new detail dumped the gruesome residue over the cliff. We resumed our former practice, leaving the stone horse-shoe and a few charred logs as an outward and visible sign of the major's diligent attention to hygiene.

Realizing that the reader, like a court, must not be wearied with cumulative proof, I mention only the deplorable incident of the colonel's inspection and pass on. Lower officers did more than enough inspecting to maintain desirable standards. The colonel's perusal was rare and was of purley ritualistic significance. No one, least of all himself, looked for or would call attention to defects, not because they weren't there, but because it would have been embarrassing. It would defeat the purpose of the ritual, just as it would for a visiting chief of state, reviewing a guard of honor, to point out a dusty shoe or a missing tunic button, or for the pope, being carried into St. Peter's, to tell a cardinal that he had his hat on backward.

The major, however, lacked a sense of occasion. He seemed unaware that in ritual, form, not substance, is of the essence, that the officers attending the colonel were there as acolytes, not fingerprint experts. As the least of the acolytes, I joined the party at the mess hall and tagged along to the cookhouse. Everything shone. The cooks, sober and in clean aprons and hats, saluted. The colonel returned their salute and murmured, "At ease," as he turned to go. The major chose this moment to hook his riding crop under a large and shining tub hanging against the wall and pull it out a few inches. He might have been Moses striking the rock. A stream of unwashed dishes and pans poured out and bounced about. The group froze as the colonel looked hard at the major and then asked our captain and first lieutenant to see him at his quarters after the inspection. He walked on.

The first necessity was profanity. Little could be added to the already exhaustive analysis of the major's failings. The shortcomings of the cooks and kitchen police hardly exceeded primitive stupidity. My own problems were not serious. Some sacrifice must be offered on the altar of discipline—passes curtailed, pay docked, and so on. But underlying opinion was clear. The real *faux pas* was the major's, and the colonel would see it that way—as he did.

Meanwhile the summer was passing. The horses' particular brand of pneumococcus seemed to lose its zest. As they recovered, they became more amenable to military discipline. Soon the drivers had the caissons rolling along; and the gunners grew proficient at mental arithmetic as they listened to the shouted numbers, twirled the wheels that moved their gun barrels, and learned to push home dummy shells, lock the breeches, and jump aside to avoid a theoretical recoil as lanyards were pulled.

South of the border the political temperature cooled as the days shortened. General Pershing came home empty-handed, rumors flew that the National Guard would be demobilized; but not before we had had a day of range practice, not before the effort and sweat of summer had been put to the test of firing live ammunition. Labor Day came and went. The mountain foliage began to turn, the blueberries to ripen on the hillsides. A few trenches were dug on a hill across a valley, enemy battery emplacements were simulated with plywood, notices were posted to warn berry pickers off the range on the chosen day. The major was posted as range officer to ride over the target area before firing began to ensure that it was clear.

On a glorious autumn morning the regiment set out for the firing position, a plateau some miles beyond our camp at the far end of the military reservation. On the parade ground the sight of the full regiment in formation was a moving one; but when Battery D brought up the end of the column of march and our rolling kitchen took its place at the end of that, martial spirit suffocated under a pall of dust. Not a breath of air moved it. Only a wet handkerchief over the nose and mouth kept lungs from filling solid.

A brief respite came when the column halted and the kitchens moved up from the tail to the head of the batteries. The drivers watered and fed their horses while the gunners ate and then took their place. Even though the major was far away on his assigned range patrol, we risked no chances with that meal—no boiled rice—there was too much live ammunition around. Not long after lunch the column debouched onto the plateau and moved straight across it. As Battery D emerged, the column broke into a trot, then swung at right angle into regimental front with guidons fluttering. When they were aligned, a bugle sent the whole command into a full gallop, a brave sight. As they reached firing position, they swung around, unlimbered guns and caissons, and took the horses, still excited and tossing their heads, to the rear.

We left the kitchen to the drivers and joined a group at the steps to a platform from which the colonel was observing the terrain through field glasses. The last preparations for firing had been completed, gun crews and officers were in their places, range finders manned. Soon officers shouted numbers as they computed distances, angles, and elevations; wheels on the guns turned. The regulation procedure from here on was pretty conventional. One or two guns would fire a long and then a short—that is, on the first they would add to the estimated range, on the second, subtract. Having thus, hopefully, bracketed the target, they would split the difference, or make other correction, and everyone would be ready for business.

The colonel turned to his second-in-command. "Range clear?" he asked with rising inflection. The words were repeated across the platform and down the steps. The words were picked up and rolled back as a receding breaker is by an incoming one. This time the inflection was reversed, assertive; not a question but an answer, "Range clear!" Then from the platform came the electrifying command: "Regimental salvo!"

The usual procedure might be conventional, but the colonel was not. He would start this exercise with a bang that few present would forget. In sixteen guns shells were shoved home, breeches slammed shut; gunners jumped clear while lanyard sergeants watched for the signal. "Fire!" said the colonel. The resultant roar was eminently satisfactory. Some of the horses snorted and gave a plunge or two. The whole hilltop across the valley burst into smoke and dust.

About a mile our side of it appeared a separate source of dust bursts, moving toward us at great speed, touching, so it seemed, only the higher mounds. An order to cease fire stopped the reloading, and field glasses centered on the speeding horseman. Word spread that it was the forgotten major. As he came nearer, he seemed to be urging the horse to greater effort. Panic or rage or both had clearly taken over. He would certainly gallop up flushed and breathing hard, fling himself from the saddle, and run toward the steps shouting, "What damned fool . . . ?" One could see him, stopped by the colonel's cold stare, salute and stammer out, "Range clear, sir!" I didn't wait for the confrontation. The platform would soon be the scene of high words, possibly controversy, in any event, unpleasantness. It was clearly no place for a mess sergeant who belonged with his field kitchen.

For a few days much talk and questioning revolved about who said what to whom. Unfortunately I could not help with this since I had rejoined the kitchen group before the dialogue began and was quite as puzzled as the others about what had happened. Anyway, it was all forgotten in a few days when we broke camp for the move home and mustering out.

Years later I met the major again. We had both exchanged military titles for somewhat higher civilian ones. But although we were to see a good deal of one

another, not always under the pleasantest circumstances, it never seemed to me that our relationship
would be improved by probing the events of that mem-
orable range practice.

Part Two **⋘**

From the Mail

A Difficult Question

Before his birth former President Truman's parents discussed the child's name, should it be a boy. For a middle name two candidates ran neck and neck. The name of each began with "S." The baby arrived before the decision, resulting in a stopgap compromise. He was christened Harry S Truman—the "S" to be filled out later. It never was. This gave rise to the quandary discussed in the following letter.

December 20, 1957

Dear Mr. President:

In your letter to me of December 5, 1957, spurred by your incurable (thank God) curiosity, you asked me this question:

Do you know the word meaning an initial standing in a name but signifying no name itself, as the "S" in

Harry S Truman?

From the Mail

You know, and so do I, how to get at a question of this sort. In my youth an advertisement used to say, "Ask the man who owns one." So I asked the two people who might know—and, of course, they were women —Elizabeth Finley, the librarian of Covington & Burling, past president of the law librarians of the country, and Helen Lally of the Supreme Court library. Their reports are enclosed.*

The essence of the matter is that we are blind men, searching in a dark room for a black hat that isn't there. The "S" in Harry S Truman (no period after the "S") does not "stand for anything." Therefore, it cannot have a descriptive noun—"vacuum," "nothing," etc., are already preempted. But, more positively, it *is* something—not representatively, but absolutely. You are "S" (without a period) because it is your name. For instance, you appointed an associate justice of the Supreme Court whose name is "Tom." Now "Tom" usually stands for "Thomas." But not in this case. There it stands, not for another more formal name, but for Tom himself.

"S" is your middle name, not a symbol, not an abbreviation, but an inseparable part of the moniker of one of the best men I have known in a largely misspent life. The same, for that matter, could be said of "Harry."

"Harry" stirs all my deepest loyalties. The senior partner, who brought me up, was christened "J. Harry Covington"; and what a man he was! After years in

---

* They both reported failure.

A Difficult Question

Congress (he was one of the men who, in 1912 in Baltimore, brought about the nomination of Woodrow Wilson), he had a phrase that to me epitomizes the political obligation, perhaps among the most honorable obligations because resting on honor alone. He never said of an obligation, "I have to do it." He always said, "I have it to do." What a vast difference! In the first, one is coerced into action; in the other, a free man assumes an obligation, freely contracted.

This has a good deal to do with politics—about which you have always thought I knew nothing—in those reaches of it which fit men for government. There are some reaches that unfit them. Honor is a delicate and tricky concept. It does not mean standing by the unfit because of friendship. But it does mean standing by in time of trouble to see a fair deal, when the smart money is taking to the bushes. All of this I learned from the old judge, and relearned again from you in unforgettable days.

So I say that "S" is a good name as it stands and I am for it. Should either of us have the good fortune to have another grandson, let's agree to persuade his parents to a middle name of just plain "S" with no period, and no explanation.

Indeed, no explanation is possible, because it is the most truly international name. In 1200 B.C. it appeared in the Phoenician as a sort of wobbly "W," but was unhappily, pronounced *sin*. By 900, in the Cretan, it looked like a 3 and had become *san,* a great improvement. For the next 500 years the 3 was turned around. Then the Latins, Irish, and Saxons, for some odd reason turned it into a "V." Finally, the British, as they have so often done, got the thing straight in a wiggle, from right to left to right, but not until our colonial ancestors, Ben Franklin included, printed it half the time as an "f" to you and me.

That again is why I like "S" for you. It has had one hell of a tempestuous life.

The Perfect Secretary

Question from a correspondent: "Having read your definition, or at least the definition you are supposed to have given, of a perfect secretary: 'She must look like a woman, think like a man, behave like a duchess, be faithful like a dog and work like an oxen' I handed it over to my secretary. Her reaction was very prompt and she asked me for your definition 'of the boss of such a secretary.' I wonder whether you could answer this question. Your simple answer: 'Me' would not be accepted."

February 24, 1956

Some enemy hath done this! I would never be so foolhardy, reckless above and beyond even a man who writes memoirs, to provoke any secretary, to say nothing of her who has held me in complete subjection for—I shall not even mention the number of years, since that might cause trouble, too. Certain sen-

57

From the Mail

ators have at one time or another hurled the charge of appeasement at me; but in the wrong field. Within the office, yes; it is the only course worthy of a man of wisdom and experience.

So I deny everything—authorship of the definition, both agreement and disagreement with it, even envy of the courage of him who made it. Mr. John W. Davis used to say that the first requisite in practising law was to have a lawyer as a partner. Even more basic is to learn that one may argue with counsel, with judges, even with clients, but never, never with one's secretary. She knows best, or, at any rate, better.

I think that I can now breathe easily again. But I won't be sure for a few days more. For this letter has to be typed!

Regarding an Analysis of
Mr. Justice Brandeis

February 27, 1956

You need never, as I am sure you know, feel any trepidation about writing to me about anything. But I for one would feel a good deal of trepidation about writing on LDB's inner nature. And for two reasons: In the first place, I would feel like saying, Brandeis is in his grave; after life's fitful fever he sleeps well. And I should have the greatest repugnance to intruding upon the citadel of that privacy he guarded so vigilantly. And to what end? Suppose he has been the subject of some undiscriminating praise. He is worthy of the urge that led to it. Suppose he had his vanities and was not proof against the constant drip of adulation. I have seen that iron man, General Marshall, be somewhat less than iron on occasion. All that

59

is so minor and unimportant, so irrelevant to what he did, to what he stood for, to the effect that he had upon the times in which he lived. There is nothing here to expose. There is no sham, or pretense, or hypocrisy lurking in the background. There is no need for a Lytton Strachey to show that the picture of *The Lady with the Lamp* left a good deal of the real Florence Nightingale out—and to overdo it, at that.

Which brings me to my second reason. A friend of mine used to have a file into which he put certain papers. It was labeled "Too Hard." I would put the project of depicting the "true" LDB into that file.

In your paper I do not see the man I knew—not so well as some others but still pretty well. And the informants you quote in the notes seem to me very wide of the mark and remote from the matters on which they testify. For instance, I am strongly persuaded that (1) Hughes's influence was a great element in keeping him on the Court, not the reverse; (2) that he withdrew from social life in Boston and Dedham because of Mrs. Brandeis's invalidism, not because he was dropped; (3) that he wrote thousands of letters, all longhand; (4) that he read a good deal of poetry; (5) that his surroundings were as they were because he wished to live a simple life as an example of revolt against excessive materialism and because the form of it was left to Mrs. Brandeis; (6) that his maturing views were his own and came from inside him and not from Mrs. Brandeis or her sisters. The opinions of Judge Hand and others are entitled to respect, but they are not mine. So often people treated LDB—par-

An Analysis of Mr. Justice Brandeis

ticularly as he became "venerable"—as an oracle and were disappointed at many of the utterances. But he could be relaxed too and could and would talk simply and even listen to gossip without pain. In short he was not an institution or an enigma, but a man, albeit a magnificently disciplined and able one. Humor could come through and fire could come through, and so could affection. But, when one finishes with all analysis and description, the likeness is still not there; and I question, again, the utility of the effort. There is enough in the public and published material for hot arguments pro and con about what he said and did without chasing the will-o-the-wisp of what went on inside and why.

This is negative help, but, I hope, not altogether useless. I just don't believe that this project has in it the possibility of success or of doing anyone any good.

President Wilson's Typewriter

Reply to a friend who asked whether our mutual friend, Justice Frankfurter, had ever seen President Wilson type.

August 27, 1959

No, Felix never saw Mr. Wilson type. But while never present at the sacrament, he once saw the chalice. It happened when as a young man he stayed over after the Taft Administration, in which he had been an assistant to Mr. Stimson, the secretary of war, to help his successor get started. He lived with a group of bachelors in a house, somewhat pretentiously called The House of Truth, which, as you can well imagine, was the center of a good deal of social gaiety. One of his friends knew Margaret Wilson; and one day she offered to give the two of them a personally conducted tour of the White House. They did the

62

state rooms downstairs and then moved on to the family quarters on the second floor, which on the continent is most confusingly called the first floor. They were shown the Oval Room, the Lincoln Room and others in a lighthearted, casual way. Finally, Miss Wilson opened a door into a small room off the Monroe Room. She pointed to a table; her voice sank to a whisper. "There," she said, "is Father's typewriter." They gazed in silence. Then the door was reverently closed.

Appeal to a Senator

December 2, 1959

While you are relaxing on your porch and watching the river flow by your door, or roaming your acres, or contemplatively absorbing a drop or two of bourbon in the cool of the evening, will you think over the request in this letter? It has to do with striking out a portion of section 1001 (f) of the National Defense Education Act of 1958.

This act, as you know, makes available to young men and women scholarships with the aid of which they can further their higher education. It is a good act and Congress deserves praise for enacting it. There is one feature of it which is causing a great deal of dissatisfaction. This dissatisfaction is not a matter of any great political importance. But it is a matter of intellectual and moral importance, and it deserves your sympathetic attention.

64

Appeal to a Senator

Section 1001 (f) requires a recipient of a government scholarship to do two things. The first is to take the Oath of Allegiance to the Constitution of the United States. This is quite proper, and no one with any sense objects to it. The other required act is an affidavit that the applicant does not believe in, and is not a member of and does not support any organization that believes in or teaches the overthrow of the United States Government by force or violence or by any illegal or unconstitutional methods. This is the requirement that is causing more and more dissatisfaction and is leading more and more colleges to withdraw from participation in the administration of the act, including the university of which I am now senior trustee; that is, Yale University.

This is a silly, futile, and insulting affidavit to require of young people engaged in preparing for their future life's work. It is quite obvious that anyone who means what he says when he swears to bear true faith and allegiance to the United States of America and to support and defend the Constitution and laws of the United States against all its enemies, foreign and domestic, does not believe in overthrowing the government by force and violence or by unconstitutional means.

I cannot believe that the federal government is truly, or should be truly, concerned about the past life and beliefs of children of eighteen. It is concerned with their future, and, as to that future, they are required to swear, as is every officer and soldier of the United States, to bear true faith and allegiance.

From the Mail

As I have said, the faculty of more and more universities, including my own, are refusing to administer the act for the reasons that I have given, and also because who knows what ephemeral organizations to which some youth may have belonged later on may be determined by someone else to be of proscribed character; because this is to insinuate that the boy or girl holds beliefs that he or she cannot hold consistent with the Oath of Allegiance; and because it raises the whole shadow of McCarthyism again.

At the last session senators [John F.] Kennedy and [Jacob] Javits attempted to rectify the situation, but did so in a clumsy sort of way, which ended in the proposal being recommitted. They started out with an amendment that would have repealed the whole section. This raised a furor about the Oath of Allegiance. They then decided to concentrate their attack on the affidavit, but in the meantime had confused everybody so much that they lost the battle.

I am sure that, if you would give your attention to this, the same group and others with your advice could do this without a commotion and to the great advantage of American education. Therefore, my dear friend, please give this more than passing thought. It is of more importance in academic halls than in Washington.

I saw that you were in town briefly to hear about the President's [Eisenhower's] travel plans and that you said he would be accompanied by our prayers. I am willing to join in your statement on the ground that I feel about the future of the United States whenever the President starts out on his travels the way the Marshal of the Supreme Court does when he opens a session of that Court. You will recall that he ends up his liturgy by saying "God save the United States for the Court is now sitting."

An Unofficial Ambassador

July 4, 1961
(What a day to write!)

Our journeys in April were most amusing and enjoyable. I went over [to Europe] on a private matter—to represent Cambodia at the International Court (with two French professors) against Thailand, represented by Sir Frank Soskice, the former British attorney general and two colleagues, one American, the other Belgian. We argued for a week on a matter of jurisdiction on which you would have stopped argument after fifteen minutes. Happily we won. Next year we go back for the merits—who owns a very ruined and very holy temple, which is right on the border.

I liked Soskice; and was as much amused as he at the procedure of speaking for ten minutes and then sitting down, out of sight behind the lectern, for ten minutes of translation into French. The Japanese judge, who understood neither, seemed a bit left out of things.

The Department of State wanted me also to talk with heads of government—where there was a government—about our ideas on strengthening conventional armaments, which seemed to be causing some concern especially in Germany and France. So the day before our argument at The Hague started I had to fly to Bonn to spend the day with the Chancellor, who was starting off on the morrow for Washington.

Although a poor way to prepare for an argument, it was a good thing that I went. The old man was full of worries and suspicions—some carefully planted in him—and these he got off his chest. Then after hours of talk, broken by lunch, walks in the garden and a game of "boccie"—bowls—he was filled up with the true gospel. "My dear friend," he said, taking my hands as I was leaving. "You have lifted a great stone from my heart." He cabled me from Washington that our day together had made his day infinitely more useful.

In The Hague and Brussels each governmental group was immersed in its own important but parochial problem—The Hague, in West New Guinea; Brussels, in the Congo. Each more than half believed, or wanted to believe, that the U.S.G., if not responsible for their troubles, could ameliorate them if it wished to. I did not have much sympathy with this point of view, and the more robust souls agreed.

In France there was de Gaulle. I had never met him before, and thought out our hour carefully in advance. Our ambassador almost ruined everything by wanting to come. But I was adamant and just refused flatly. (I remembered Brandeis's form of ending discussion of a refusal. "So that you may know," he would write, "that my decision is final, I give no reasons.") I was determined to keep the initiative and not argue with de Gaulle. The form chosen was to say that President Kennedy had asked me in preparation for his meeting with the General to lay before him the recommendations for U.S. policy toward Europe that I had made to the President. It worked like a charm. I knew that half the stuff he would hate, but it was good for him to hear it straight and in tentative form.

The General is impressive. He has the authentic grand manner. I was received with a grave courtesy that would have befitted Louis XIV himself. We exchanged compliments in an eighteenth-, or probably seventeenth-century, solemnity and went to work. One exchange pleased us both. I was proposing the NATO Council as a central point for allied consultation to try to make the Alliance function with some approach to the speed and decisiveness of the Kremlin. Of course, he wants all decisions made by the U.S., U.K., and France, the others being merely told. So he stopped me and said, "But will it work?"

"Who knows," I answered, "until we really try it?"

"But it is illogical," he persisted. "NATO was conceived as a military alliance, now you are trying to make it a political mechanism."

"Quite right," I said. "We Americans think less of logic in politics than you French do. With us the test is whether something works. If it does, logic conforms to a new verity." This, he conceded was a point of view.

I finished the interview in just fifty-eight minutes by the clock behind him, rose, and was on my way out before his *chef de cabinet* opened the door to expedite withdrawal. An interesting hour. On the military parts he listened intently and asked good questions for enlightenment, not controversy.

Fanfani in Rome was not much. No one since de Gasperi has seemed to be. But Italy, as usual, produced a full quota of interest. We started off at a "meeting of intellectuals" from all over Europe at Bologna, where we had never been before, the Il Mulino Conference. Il Mulino is one of Italy's greatest publishing houses, a center of liberalism of the Italian type, and apparently well off. So many things were delightful. Italian oratory, D. H. Lawrence, in *Twilight in Italy* says, operates directly on the blood without any confusing interpolation of intellectual content. Listening without the earphones was much better. One got the full sonorous flow of sound, without being disturbed by schoolmarmish twittering of the English interpreters trying to make sense out of it all.

Then there was Senator Medici's telling us that the Italians were pleasant civilized people but not worth bothering about. "We are tired and played out," he said. "Only you and the Russians have energy enough to struggle any more." Yes, his family was an old one from the modern point of view, but really newcomers from the long view of Italian history.

"People," he said, "ask my friend, Senator Maximo,

From the Mail

'Are you really descended from Fabius Maximus?' And he replies wearily, 'Such was the tradition at the time of Christ.' "

Well, we had two and a half days of meetings, oratory, and very pleasant lunches and dinners with some interesting people. Just the same, I wouldn't count too heavily on the Italians if the going got tough. They just aren't made for heavy or nervous work. But they are invaluable to have around.

Our Venice visit was great fun and a disappointment, too. The Giustiniani library * turned out to be largely sixteenth century of which there is a plethora. The eleventh-, twelfth-, and thirteenth-century documents, of which there were very few, were largely religious disputation—transubstantiation, pro and con, etc. The foundation did not think it worth further investment. So, alas, we had to close a promising chapter.

But with our Venetian friends we added new ones and had a delightful time, including a beautiful afternoon in the garden on the Giudecca of King Alexander (of Greece's) widow—an enchanted spot, if ever I saw one—and a glorious lunch at Torcello. All too soon we were headed home and into a new assignment on Berlin, a worrisome one.

---

* The library of Count Giustiniani, whose family had been for many centuries in Venetian trade, contained a great quantity of unexamined documents. I obtained a grant from a foundation to have them examined by scholars to learn whether they might throw light on trade in the Middle Ages. [D.A.]

What Makes a Great Nation

Reply to a member of the sixth grade, Ridge Road School, Paramus, New Jersey.

November 20, 1962

To discuss why the U.S.A. is a "great nation," as you invite me to do, we must understand what we mean—or ought to mean, if we use the word correctly—by a "great nation." "Great" carries the notion of magnitude. It is the opposite of small. It has nothing to do with our approval or disapproval of a nation, or with the virtue or wickedness of its policies from the viewpoint of other nations. So, as much as one might admire the qualities of the Dutch, Israeli, or Lebanese people, they are not citizens of great nations. On the other hand, the Soviet Union, as much as it threatens our most cherished values, is a great nation.

Now going back to the suggestion that magnitude is

73

close to the essence of greatness in a nation, the following are vital factors:

Population—its size, character, and skill;

Resources—the extent and quality of natural resources and productive plant;

Technology—its present state and the quality and rate of its development;

Will—the vigor, coherence, and direction of the national consensus.

Most of these elements and their importance are almost self-evident. When I speak of the "character" of a population, I am thinking of what Milton had in mind when he said, "Citizens, it is no small matter what manner of men ye are!" Indeed, it is not a small matter at all. It is an essential matter.

Under the last element, will, comes everything that enables a people to act together with vigor and decisiveness, and—as de Tocqueville put it—"to persevere in a great design." If you wish to observe the deterioration of a gifted state through fragmentation and irresolution of will, I recommend Thucydides' *Peloponnesian War,* a very great book.

All of these four elements have played a tremendous part in the development of the greatness of America.

Perhaps to your surprise I have not mentioned forms of government or the role of law as elements in the greatness of a nation. In our case the Judaic, Greco-Roman, Anglo-Saxon traditions blended in our heritage to produce an important result, both in liberating dynamic individual vigor and in restraining the power of the state and the dominant (from time to time) element in our society during our three-hundred-year struggle to develop this half-continent.

But do not forget that the Soviet Union achieved greatness without these traditions, as did China and Japan. Spain in the fifteenth and sixteenth centuries and France in the seventeenth and eighteenth centuries achieved greatness with only some of them.

The effect of ethical considerations would be even more difficult to appraise.

So you see your inquiry, if rigorously pursued, will lead into a good deal more than the praise of great men and the cataloguing of virtues.

Suggestion for an Article

March 12, 1964

Your delightful piece on the troubles a colonial power has in pushing its fledgings out of the nest and keeping them out did, as you suspected, amuse me a lot.

Why don't you do another on what a terrible time those well-meaning old codgers, John Bull and Uncle Sam, are having in maintaining *pieds-à-terre* around the world in these nice friendly new countries, which are the hope of the future. The trouble all comes from the habit of exuberant youngsters in burning the places down, or, if they are more moderate, just sacking them, whenever the poor arthritic old fellows

76

don't move as fast or in the direction that our young friends think they should. It would not be anything to worry about except for the cost, because quite clearly we are only going through the cycle that Charles Lamb pointed out in the roasting of pigs. The delights of roast pig were first discovered by an accidental fire. For a while incendiarism became the accustomed method of roasting until the heat was more economically contained. Perhaps until these hopes of the future learn to read and write and use plumbing, we ought to have symbolic embassies, which they could burn down as a ritualistic protest. We might even learn from this that it wasn't necessary to have any embassies.

At any rate, the idea is yours.

Appreciation for an Author

To Lady Violet Bonham-Carter about her book, *Winston Churchill As I Knew Him.*

May 9, 1965

Your note followed by your splendid book have put me deeply in your debt. Lord Attlee is far too timid in saying that your book is "quite possibly a classic." There is no "quite possibly" about it. It is a classic.

For days I have been absorbed in it with delight. A live book, a sparkling book, a penetrating political history, and an equally penetrating and also a loving and just personal appraisal. How rarely these two qualities go together.

Devotion, loyalty, and justice, or the preservation of the critical faculty seem to be able to coexist only in Great Britain. With us loyalty seems to require the total submergence of the critical faculty. If one says here that Mr. Truman, whom many of us adore, was a great, perhaps very great, President, but are hesitant to add that he was or is a great man, mutual friends become uneasy. Our superlative demands all superlatives. And so our heroes tend to look like our statues.

But you can and do write of Sir Winston's mistakes with as clear recognition of them as of his brave and farseeing acts of statesmanship. You give us the whole man, warts and all.

What a portrait it is! And painted against a great political background. The last years in the last country since the Greece and Athens of Pericles when so few men of great abilities and great qualities as civilized men controlled the destinies of the globe.

To me it was a basically tragic time. Their excellence, their brilliance, their Homeric battles were all on the surface. The real currents of life and power and—if one dares be mystical—of destiny ran deeper than their thoughts, their apprehensions and intuitions. They were borne along unknowing to the cataract. This really was the Twilight of the Gods.

You have brought it all back and made it all live for me again as no one else has—or, I am sure, will.

Your second chapter on Gallipoli, the land operation, is almost too poignant to finish. Like the story of the Crucifixion, one knows too well how it will end.

What I have written thus far omits the joy of what Felix Frankfurter used to call the "nuggets" you leave all through your pages.

That when very young you "knew that politics depend above all else upon the power of persuading others to accept ideas." So many have gone to their doom believing that the true essence was the ability to be elected;

and your observation—so reminiscent to me of Louis Brandeis—that WSC "never fell a victim to the black magic of specialist infallibility";

and your remark that Eddie Marsh "discharged his civil service duties with punctilious perfection, meticulous accuracy, and the complete absense of mind we bring to Bradshaw when we look up trains for other people";

and your recollection of the Master of Balliol describing Lloyd George as having "religious fervour without moral perception";

and Maynard's view of Lloyd George, "When he is alone in a room there is no one there"; and so on.

Your pages are full of such as these. Sheer delights requiring an appreciative audience to hear each read aloud.

To do all this in your first book just is not fair to mankind who grubs along jealous of winged minds. But the joy you bring your readers—and particularly this one—should in any sound literary theological system bring you absolution for the sin of brilliance.

Thank you so very much.

Thoughts Written to a British Friend on the Assassination of President Kennedy

December 10, 1963

This nation was truly shattered by the radio and television on November 22. Its mood then and thereafter was not what the announcers, chewing an endless conventional cud until after the funeral, have reported it to be. Surely there was sorrow for the death of a brave young man and an inexpressibly gallant young widow and two utterly pathetic and heartbreaking children. It was not bewilderment at the loss of a great and tried leader, as with FDR, for JFK was not that. It was fear from the utter collapse of all sense of security which lay at the bottom of the emotion. No one knew what had happened. We were like victims of an earthquake. Even the ground under our feet was shaking. There was no security. Who had

From the Mail

killed the President? A fanatical Southerner? A demented Negro? A right-wing fascist? What was likely to follow? More violence? More deaths? Where was Johnson?

It all conspired to produce a terrifying shock. We had grown unused to the emotion of fear since World War II. We never are used to the great place in all our lives that the President fills. This is—though we rarely realize it—a presidential system. He is the *whole* establishment—monarch, parliament, Bank of England, archbishop, the whole thing. We are used to treating him with disrespect and changing him ourselves for irrelevant reasons. If he is old and should die of a heart attack, as Ike might have, we would be upset. But where in the person of a young and vibrant man he becomes a corpse within an hour, the vast factor of chance and insecurity in all our separate lives as well as our collective life becomes oppressive and paralyzingly terrifying.

People wanted to be alone and to be quiet. We were all, quite possibly, in the grip of some vast unthinkable to which as Judge Holmes said, every predicate was an impertinence. The numinous quality of fate was in the air. The vast lines filing by the casket were on a pilgrimage of propitiation.

From this state of shock we were rescued in part by the resilience of this nation, and in part by Lyndon Johnson. There was never a moment of doubt that he was in command. With sensitivity and talk he led the nation in proper but not mawkish mourning. When the funeral was ended, he assumed charge of headquarters.

To a Librarian on Reading

March 1, 1966

Dear Madam Librarian:

You ask what reading has meant to me. Until you asked, I had never asked myself. Reading has been as much a part of living as thinking, as necessary as breathing. I cannot remember when I was not reading. To stop reading would be a sort of partial death—the death of all of me which extends beyond what I can see, hear, taste, or touch, pretty much the whole life of the mind.

Never to have read would have killed even more than that, for what one has read enters into the life of the mind as much as what one has experienced. Indeed, it gives experience a good deal of its meaning by apprehending it in the light thrown by the experience of others. It heightens consciousness, awareness, which is what, so I understand, differentiates man from the other animals.

From the Mail

Whether one reads verse, novels, essays, history, or biography, one learns that experiences which might be thought unique are not so; one learns how others thought, acted, and felt under the same circumstances. In short, one has the experience of emotion innumerable times and in innumerable ways. Reading is living.

Part Three ⋘

On Public Service

Voice of Experience

"Fortunately, there is no disposition in this country to search for scapegoats to blame for the situation (in Vietnam). Americans are singularly free from the disposition to vent a sanguinary fury on officials who have the misfortune to preside at disagreeable affairs . . ." [From a *Washington Post* editorial, July 10, 1965.]

To the Washington Post:

I read that here exists no disposition
    To seek for scapegoats for a situition.
Americans, you say, are singularly free
    From any wish "to vent a sanguinary
Fury on officials who, alas, preside
    At disagreeable affairs" at ebb of tide.
Reading, as always, at your bidding,
    I wonder who the hell you're kidding.

87

On Public Service

(With salute to Ogden Nash)

Seeking narcotic help in wassail,
    "I caught the eye of one small fossil,
'Cheer up, sad world,' he said, and winked.
'It's kind of fun to be extinct'."

DEAN ACHESON

The Washington Post, July 14, 1965.

88

The Test of Happiness

Your memorandum on the importance of interesting students of secondary schools in government, with your request for my comments, has come to me.

I am all for young (and also old) men of quality going into public life and government service. But why do they have to be "dedicated" men? To dedicate means to set aside for the service of a divine being or for a sacred use. Secondarily, it means to set aside for any definite use. In this sense men who go into public service are, of course, dedicated to it by going into it. The word is redundant. Used as a color or image word to suggest Sir Galahad, it is worse than confusing. There is nothing divine or sacred about public service, any more than about dentistry.

Letter to a friend who requested comments on a memorandum; *The New York Times*, February 2, 1958, Mr. James Reston's column.

89

On Public Service

Both are important. There have been times in my life when a dentist seemed to me more important than the President or the Pope. But because we *need* dentists or doctors, or scientists, or bomber pilots is not a compelling reason why any of my grandsons should become one, or why their schoolmasters should try to steer them toward one of these careers. And yet I would be eager to see them steered toward a career, perhaps a life, of public service, as some of their ancestors were. Why? Not because I see the gleam of a halo forming about their heads, but because there is no better or fuller life for a man of spirit. The old Greek conception of happiness is relevant here: "The exercise of vital powers along lines of excellence, in a life affording them scope."

This is the Geiger counter that tells us where to dig. It explains also why to everyone who has ever experienced it the return from public life to private life leaves one feeling flat and empty. Contented, interested, busy—yes. But exhilarated—no. For one has left a life affording scope for the exercise of vital powers along lines of excellence. Not the only one, I am sure. Undoubtedly Einstein, Michelangelo, Savonarola, Shakespeare, and a good many others could give interesting testimony on other lives. But outside of aesthetics and teaching—religion belongs to both—the requirement of "scope" is hard to come by in this age, outside of public life. Surely vital powers are exercised in the whole vast task of feeding, clothing, housing us, as I am sure Mr. McElroy was aware in making soap and being handsomely paid for it. But I am equally sure that he now feels a zest, a sense that the only limitation upon the exercise of all his vital powers is his own capacity, that he never felt before.

I am in danger, perhaps, of overstating my point. So I do not want to draw a picture of public life as a perpetual marijuana jag, or to leave out its colossal obstacles, some of them killers, as not a few of our close friends have found out. But, painted with all the warts, it is a life of scope for the exercise of all one's vital powers, even though one may become a casualty in exercising them.

This has not always been true. For instance, in Athens of the fifth century (B.C.) public life offered the greatest scope for men of talent in all Greek history; in the fourth century, after the defeat and humiliation of Athens, it presented none. In the last half of the nineteenth century, public life in England reached its most luxuriant and brilliant flowering, while in America it sank to depths not plumbed before or since. It did so because in this country the real scope for the exercise of vital powers (perhaps not altogether in the direction of excellence) lay in exploiting a continent and building industrial and financial empires as glittering as dreams of Cathay. Today much of the glitter and the semblance of the rewards (the reality is hidden in expense accounts and management participation plans) still exists, but the power, and with it the scope for action, of business and finance have faded with the rise of the dangers and the demands of a two-camp world. Today, more than ever before, the prize of the general is not a bigger tent, but command. The managers of industry and finance have the bigger tents; but command rests with govern-

On Public Service

ment. Command, or, if one prefers, supreme leadership, demands and gives scope for the exercise of every vital power a man has in the direction of excellence.

How, then, does one present to the boys at your school a life of public service? Not, I am sure, as an evangelist appealing to the young squires to turn their backs on the world and dedicate themselves to a sort of secular order for ministering to the peasants, nor as crusaders led by Mr. Nixon to bring Communist infidels to capitalism or the sword. Rather, I think, one educates them to know the world in which they live, to understand that government will go on whether they take part in it or not, that command is too important to be entrusted to the ignorant, even though they may be well-meaning and dedicated, and to an understanding of the good life, of happiness as the Greeks saw it, of the joy of exercising vital powers in a life affording them scope, of the limitless scope of governmental responsibilities. In addition, they might learn, as an authority on the process of revolution has pointed out, that "Brave men are not uncommon in any system, but there is a tendency in most systems to make courage and a disciplined openness of mind to the significant facts mutually exclusive. This is the immediate cause of the downfall of every ruling class that ever falls."

Against a background of this sort I wholly agree that visits of public men can do much to sharpen and focus images of a world not yet experienced, and possibly— though not probably—give an occasional boy the sort of hero that TR was to me.

Public Service

What I want you to think about with me this afternoon is: What is in the work which we are all doing together which has made a person devote willingly and enthusiastically and eagerly fifty years of her life to this work? What is it that makes each one of us every day, day in and day out, work eagerly and enthusiastically and loyally and devotedly at what we are doing? Why is it that every time I go home—I think I stay much too late at the Department of State—I find that there are scores of other people who are staying later than I have stayed? I see lights all over the building. Sometimes when I get home and want to talk to one of my colleagues and telephone him at his home I

Made before employees of the Department of State at the Third Annual Awards Ceremony in the Departmental Auditorium, Washington, D. C., on Oct. 18, 1951; *Department of State Bulletin* Vol. XXV, October 29, 1951.

find he isn't there at all, he is still at the Department. I find that my colleagues and all of you give up your holidays, give up your evenings, give up your weekends to stay and work on projects which have fired your imagination. Sometimes I have to order my colleagues to get out of that building, to go away and stay away for a few days, and I find, as many Secretaries of State have found before me, that no one pays the slightest bit of attention to these orders. What is it that fires this whole wonderful outfit of which we are all parts?

We know certain things that it most certainly is not. It isn't any desire for applause or popularity or power, because it takes a very short time for all of us to find out that that just isn't in the cards for people who work in the State Department. It isn't that. It certainly isn't any great material reward. It is not always clear that all of us are going to get any reward. However that may be, perhaps that was unduly crystal. We do not find that a long career in the State Department leads to being listed among the fifty richest men and women in the United States. So it isn't that. What is it then?

It seems to me that what it is is the chance to serve your country and to serve it as part of an outfit of which you can be proud, where you can be happy, where you can know that your colleagues feel the same way about it that you do, and you know that you can trust and be trusted all the way through. It is a chance to serve. It is the same sort of thing in this Department which creates great military outfits, groups of men who have lived together and fought together and have pride in their organization. That, I think, is why it is that this Department is so great.

I have been in other departments of the government. I have been in Washington for over thirty years and I don't think any of my colleagues in the cabinet would think it amiss of me if I said that after having worked for eleven years in the Department of State I think it is the finest outfit in the entire government. I don't think any of my distinguished predecessors would think in any way that I was reflecting upon prior administrations if I said that the State Department today is better than it ever has been in its long and great history. I think they would feel that of course it should be, that if it ever stopped making progress, if it ever stopped meeting from year to year the increasing demands upon it, then it would be slipping back.

No organization can stay static. It has to move forward or it has to move backward, and the Department has been moving, I am glad and delighted to say, further and faster ahead every year. The responsibilities laid upon us are enormous, tremendous responsibilities, and we have grown to meet those with each new added responsibility.

Now this view which we have of ourselves, which I do not think is the conceited view, is not shared by everybody. There are people who have other views about the Department of State, and those people are by no means shy in expressing them. I should be the last one to be tender about criticism. I criticize the Department of State, I like to be criticized by my colleagues and by anybody who understands what they are talking about. Criticism is good for us. The very fact that criticism is going on means that the people of the United States are interested in what we are doing. If they weren't interested they wouldn't talk about it and we wouldn't be criticized, but they know how important what we are doing is for the country.

Many people have ideas, many of the ideas are well-informed, some of them are not, but at any rate they are all expressed and that leads to debate as to whether we are doing the right thing or should do something different. That is all to the good and I have no objection about that at all.

But the other thing is very different from that, and that is criticism which springs from narrow political motives, criticism which is reckless and heedless of the national interest, criticism which is directed to untrue attacks on the personal character and the personal loyalty and devotion of many among us. Those are different, those attacks we need have no patience with. We need not regard them as even decent expressions of American public opinion. Those attacks tear down the confidence of the country in the whole structure of government. They are evil, so far as the country is concerned, and we might just as well state that clearly and understand that that is our attitude toward that sort of criticism. There is no use saying that that type of criticism has done us no harm. It has done us a lot of harm, a great deal of harm.

This year we held, as we always do, examinations for the Foreign Service. The number of applicants to take those examinations was just half what it was two years ago. This seemed to us to be a large decline. So we went to the schools and colleges from which these applicants came and asked why it was that there had been such a decline in those who wanted to take the examinations for the Foreign Service. We were told that the major reason was directly traceable to these vicious personal attacks, and we were told that the unwillingness of young men and women to subject themselves to that sort of attack led to these promising young people turning this year to other opportunities which were open to them instead of, as they have in the past so often, to enter the Foreign Service.

Now there are other ways where this sort of attack has hurt us. There are other ways which are more subtle than what I have just mentioned. That it hurt us, there is no question about that. One thing, however, it has not hurt. It has not hurt our self-respect and it has not hurt our determination to do our duty. It has not hurt our determination to do it with everything we have in us.

The sort of thing we have been subjected to isn't at all new in the world. In the sixteenth century Machiavelli was writing about how to accomplish certain results that you wanted to accomplish, and in his discourses he says, "Amongst the other means which ambitious citizens frequently employed to achieve power was this practice of calumniating." Well, if this was a racket in the sixteenth century it certainly had something of a revival in the twentieth century. But, as I say, the way to meet this is to meet it by doing our duty, and if we continue to do our duty, if we continue to hold our heads high, it will pass.

The American people are fair people. They won't stand forever this sort of vicious personal scurrilous attack. They won't stand for it and if we just go ahead steadily doing our duty, carrying on as the department has always carried on in the past, then those young people who have been temporarily discouraged from joining us will see that this is the one place in the world that they simply must join, because here is devotion, here is character, here is the opportunity to serve the country. And I think that each of us can meet the sort of attacks I have just been talking about by every day saying "I am going to do my duty today in such a way that I will know that these attacks are the lies which I am sure they are." If everybody does that we don't have to worry. We will come through this period.

Not all of us can do dramatic things; not all of us can do things that people talk about, but each one of us has his duty and each one of us can do that.

Justice Holmes talks in one of his little speeches about the feelings of a man who has come to the end of a very long life and a long service on the bench and looks back over what he has done and finds it so distressingly small, and he ends up by saying words that I should like to leave with you. He said, "Alas, gentlemen, we cannot live our dreams. We are lucky enough if we can give a sample of our best and if we can know in our hearts that it was nobly done."

The Critical Spirit

A commencement speaker in the year of our
Lord one thousand nine hundred and forty-six is in a
quandary. He brings with him enough precepts, in all
conscience, but when he comes to set up these sign-
posts at the crossroads he is not too sure where the
roads lead and how the signs ought to point.

Mr. Lilienthal in his fine book about the TVA tells
of the motorist in the Tennessee hills who stopped to
ask his way to Jonesville. His informant embarked
three or four times—and confidently enough—on de-
tailed and complicated directions, only to abandon
each effort. Finally he said "Mister, if I was going to
Jonesville, I certainly wouldn't start from here."

We can all sympathize with that sentiment. Cer-

Address to the graduating class of Bryn Mawr College, Bryn Mawr,
Pennsylvania, June 11, 1946; *Department of State Press Release No.
397.*

99

tainly none of us would willingly re-create the circumstances under which you and the whole country and the whole world face the problems of your lives and the lives and fortunes of all of us everywhere. We know —if we may both shift the metaphor and shift from Mr. Lilienthal to Mr. Chesterton—that we are all in the same boat, and that we are all seasick. But that is no reason for pulling a long face or losing heart. Seasickness is rarely fatal. Others are in far worse plight than we. From time immemorial when people believe these two things they are on the verge of effort; and with effort we have made a start.

A good way to make a start is to survey the assets which one has and then the most immediate problems one faces and to see how to use what one has in order to do what has to be done.

You graduates of 1946 have two great assets. Nearly all your adult lives you have been learning discipline, learning to live with uncertainty and anxiety, learning how terrible a judgment can fall upon error—no matter how well intentioned—and how robust a combination of intelligence and effort is the price of survival. The experience of the past six years has been a hard school but its diploma will stand you in good stead.

Then, the diplomas you receive today certify, among many other things, that you have had developed in you the critical spirit. Graduates of Bryn Mawr do not, certainly they should not, bow before the printed word. They do not have to read a favorite columnist or the latest poll to know how to form a judgment. Judgment is formed upon the evidence, all the evidence, and this means the critical appraisal of the testimony of many witnesses and many documents. Moreover it is a continuing judgment, and a judgment which, like a compass, has to be corrected against the magnetic effect of our own will to fashion the result.

When we turn to the problems we face, many of us at once look abroad. Foreign affairs have become an absorbing interest. This is natural and right, but this interest should not obscure the pressing and immediate problem of conducting our own affairs.

We cannot have a sustained and useful influence abroad if we become divided, confused, and futile at home.

I should like to discuss this aspect of our affairs in the light of a fact which I think has escaped the attention it deserves. This is understandable, since we all have more to worry about than even a good worrier can handle.

The fact I ask you to think about is this. A democratic system subjected to severe external pressure and danger is deprived of one of the elements which in the past has played a large part in its operation—the element of time.

Throughout our history we have been very fortunate in that we have had time to argue things out, to make mistakes, to get into messes, to learn by trial and error, to get used to new conditions gradually. In other words, we have been able to do very well by putting most of our attention on our individual affairs. We have not been forced by dangers from the outside to concentrate upon public affairs with discipline, organization, a pressing realization that our common interests are more essential than our separate interests, and with an appreciation of the importance of intelligence.

The experience of the 1930s ought to convince us that this element of plenty of time is no longer available. If the reference seems inconclusive, I cite the atomic bomb, guided missiles, and biological warfare, as the instruments by which external pressure has deprived us of time.

This does not mean that our system is not sound and workable. It does mean that it must become—which means that we must become—more competent, more disciplined, and more absorbed in our common interests and in what we do about them.

All that we can and should do is far beyond my wisdom. But it is possible to give some illustrations.

We have recently seen the industrial life of the country crippled, if not stopped, on successive occasions because labor and management, unable to agree, broke off their common effort. No sensible person believes that the crucial issues were in any sense vital enough to warrant the disaster which followed to the country as a whole. Yet these harms were allowed to happen, partly because the men in control on both sides were not able or willing to stop them, and, partly, because the rest of us will not think enough and do enough about these matters except in times of crises. We can no longer afford this luxury of indifference. There is no longer the time to deal with these affairs in this way.

Then we turn to processes of government at both

ends of Pennsylvania Avenue. The problem is the same; the manifestations different. Our machinery was devised for a government which was thought of as soldier, policeman, umpire. It is actually engaged in functions of management—and has to be. To do this Congress must lay down in many fields the general principles and rules which shall govern, leaving to others the administrative details.

This takes all the time and study which all the five hundred-odd members can give. But no sooner is a general statute enacted, than Congress becomes involved in the very administrative detail which it knows it cannot handle. A special investigating committee is set up to go into every last act of the administrative agency; or, if this is not done, the appropriation committees will spend weeks and often months attempting to direct administration through the qualifying or withholding of funds.

And not content with the troubles which the Lord sends, the Congress adds to them by the practice of putting a time limit on legislation, so that it has to regurgitate and chew its cud annually or biennially. This is useful in an obstacle race, but not as an improvement in modern democratic method.

At our own end of the Avenue, we have problems in method also. Today every matter with which government must deal is, to use the figure of Justice Holmes, a bird on the wing. The task is to focus a single eye on that bird. We have any number of departmental and agency policies, but how to get, within measurable time, a government policy—even an executive government policy—has so far eluded us.

In our system the cabinet is a collective noun to describe a number of administrative officials. It is not an institution. Under the presidential system the problem is one of organization, not insoluble or over-difficult, but not yet solved. We shall not be very maneuverable until it is. And when time is short maneuverability is important.

Then also we have the media of public information —the press and the radio. They, too, need self-discipline and a sense of the community of interest. I suppose that nowhere in the world is the news reported so fully and fairly as in this country. But unhappily we do not stop there. A very large part of our effort is spent in reporting events before they happen—this is called a scoop—or in speculating upon the purposes or motives of persons involved, or in reporting gossip or trivia so that the reader may peep through the keyhole and be on the "inside."

The net result of this gloss, upon an otherwise outstanding system of public information, is to get people fighting with one another—to precipitate controversies in every direction—and to make the end product of the democratic process—agreement—considerably more difficult. There is no time for this sort of private impediment to the common task.

These are illustrations, not a catalogue. They are troubles that we can remedy ourselves. Here we are not impeded by the difficulty of reaching agreement with other peoples with different traditions, institutions, languages, and purposes. They are among the things that must be remedied if our system is going to be capable of recognizing and dealing with forces and events originating from the outside.

Every horseman knows the difference in a tight spot between a horse which is collected and one which is not and cannot be. It may be the difference between coming a cropper or not. It means the difference between controlled and instant response to any eventuality and blundering. There is no reason why we cannot school ourselves to be collected.

If we will do this, the rewards will be very great. We shall have taken the most important single step open to us to preserve individual freedom in this world as well as to preserve our own national existence as a free people. We shall also reap unexpected benefits in the world at large. For our influence will be greatly magnified and improved as we increase our capacity to direct it wisely, exercise it promptly, and support it powerfully.

Thoughts about Thought
in High Places

Last June, President Eisenhower made the commencement speech to the first graduating class of the Senior Foreign Officers School.

"In the years that Secretary Dulles and I served together," he said, "he often spoke about the lack of opportunity of high officers of government, and indeed of high officers of any profession, for contemplation. He felt so strongly about this that he believed that there should be some reorganization in the very highest echelons of the executive departments so that there could be more time to think about the job."

When I read this my mind flew to the signs which, for a time, hung on the walls of some offices, urging "THINK"—and the addendum written in pencil on

The New York Times Magazine, October 11, 1959.

Thoughts about Thought in High Places

one of them, "OR THWIM." For this pungent alternative seemed to me to go to the heart of the problem of contemplation in the executive departments.

These departments are meant to be what they are called—"executive" departments, that is, agencies of action. Contemplation, in these departments, is not an end in itself; it is a means to action—the wisest action under the circumstances, to be sure, but action. What is needed is not, as the President said, "to think about the job"—that is for professors and columnists—but to think about what to do and how to do it. In the executive departments salvation lies only in works.

Now it happens that Secretary Dulles also talked with me on this subject. He had come to the department in response to my invitation to arrange an orderly transfer of responsibility. He told me that he was not going to work as I had done, but would free himself from involvement with what he referred to as personnel and administrative problems, in order to have more time to think.

I did not comment, but was much struck by the conjunction of ideas. I wondered how it would turn out. For it had been my experience that thought was not of much use without knowledge and guidance, and that who should give me both and how competent they would be must depend on who chose, dealt with, assigned and promoted these people, and established the forms of organization within which they worked. All this seemed a precondition of thinking which I could not ignore if my thoughts were going to amount to anything.

On Public Service

So the President's commencement speech has nagged at me. This absorption with the Executive as Emerson's "Man Thinking," surrounded by a cabinet of Rodin statues, bound in an oblivion of thought, chin on fist, elbow on knee, seemed to me unnatural and unnecessary. Surely thinking is not so difficult, so hard to come by, so solemn as all this.

Isn't the problem, I have wondered, a little different? Doesn't it involve a choice of what the "very highest echelons," the President and the cabinet, spend their time on, and of finding ways of making available to them the right information to think with and about? Executives should not be encouraged to spin thoughts and policies out of their own viscera as spiders spin their webs.

It is hard to get reliable data on the matters which now occupy the time of "the very highest echelons." Of course, they vary with the men involved, their physical and mental vitality, their powers of concentration, their resources of knowledge, experience, and wisdom. Their tasks are difficult ones. This cannot be altered. Our present question is: Is their time well spent? If not, is the remedy "reorganization in the very highest echelons"?

The most available data we have, skimpy and inadequate as it is, is the daily announcement of the President's appointments. For the first and last weeks of July, typical weeks, they appear in a list at the end of this piece.

No one knows better than I that the published appointment list of the President or a cabinet officer is only that one-tenth of the iceberg which appears above water. But even a short study of the sample given makes two points clear: first, at least half the appointments are wholly unnecessary; and, second, those which are necessary are neither very time-consuming nor exhausting.

One other matter needs to be stressed in any consideration of time for contemplation—the long weekends in Maryland and Pennsylvania in carefully preserved seclusion from run-of-the-mill concerns. This is wise and proper. All through the war, President Roosevelt, as those who have read William Hassett's delightful *Off the Record With FDR* know, sought refuge at Hyde Park from the insistent pressures of Washington and there achieved the essential prerequisite of contemplation, relaxation. One can think under pressure, but not contemplate. Ruminants lie down to ruminate.

So I suggest again that perhaps the problem is both not so great and greater than has been imagined. Not so great, in that there is time enough both to think and to contemplate if the highest echelons do not give in to the human desire, shared by the lower echelons, to avoid the pain of thought by escape to something less exacting, like routine or going somewhere. And the problem is greater because the world's and the nation's problems today are so complex, tough, and recalcitrant as to blunt the sharpest thought. This means that they are not likely to yield to any amount of reorganization of the thinkers.

The military substitute for thought at the top is

staff. Staff is of great importance. It performs the indispensable function of collecting the food for thought, appraising and preparing it. It is the means of carrying out decisions made. But, when it also performs the function of final thought, judgment and decision, then there is no top—only the appearance of one. This can happen in a number of ways, but the most insidious, because it seems so highly efficient, is the "agreed" staff paper sent up for "action," a euphemism for "approval."

"One can always," I have said elsewhere, "get an agreed paper by increasing the vagueness and generality of its statements. The staff of any interdepartmental committee has a fatal weakness for this type of agreement by exhaustion." But a chief who wants to perform his function of knowing the issues, the factors involved and their magnitudes, and of deciding, needs, where there is any doubt at all, not agreed papers, but disagreed papers.

Original thought on the frontiers of knowledge is, as Professor Percy Bridgman has pointed out, a lonely and individual process. But the thought of a chief of a government department or of a government itself does and should involve others. I have already suggested part of the reason why, but only part. Popular conceptions about government are in large part interesting folklore; and the instinct of the bureaucracy for self-preservation and the egotism of the chiefs perpetuate it. One of these concepts is that "policy" originates at the top and is passed down.

Thoughts about Thought in High Places

To be sure, *great decisions* are, for the most part, made at the top, when they are not made by events. But, as for policy—the sum total of many decisions—it must be said, as it has been said of sovereignty, that its real sources are undiscoverable. One fact, however, is clear to anyone with experience in government: The springs of policy bubble up; they do not trickle down.

When this upsurgence of information, ideas, and suggestions is vigorous, appreciated, and encouraged, strong, imaginative, and effective policies are most apt to result. When the whole function of determining what is what, and what to do about it, is gathered into one hand, or into a small group at the top, the resulting action may or may not be strong, but it is likely to be ill-adapted to reality and self-defeating.

What has just been said underlines the judicial element in the function of headship and the great importance of interplay between head and staff at all stages in the development of decisions. By this I mean that the chief must from time to time familiarize himself with the whole record; he must consider opposing views, put forward as ably as possible. He must examine the proponents vigorously and convince them that he knows the record, is intolerant of superficiality or of favor-seeking, and not only welcomes but demands criticism.

As General Marshall said at the beginning of his secretaryship, when I asked what he expected of me as what he called his chief of staff, "First, the most unvarnished truth, particularly about myself. I have no feelings"—then added—"except those which I reserve for Mrs. Marshall." And he never faltered in this attitude.

Through this judicial function, through pondering what has been read and heard, and a suggestion or decision that one of several lines is the one to be pursued, the chief makes his most valuable contribution to thought and policy. It takes work and it takes time.

It also requires orderly procedure. Meetings should be as small as possible. Anyone who needs or permits platoons of aides to accompany him brands himself as incompetent. All parties in interest should be present at the same time, should have their say and hear what is said by all others. They should also hear the decision, which should be in writing or recorded. This, I am sure, seems disappointingly simple. But it is disappointingly rare.

All readers of Sir Arthur Bryant's *The Turn of the Tide* (based on the war diaries of Lord Alanbrooke, Chief of the British Imperial General Staff) will recall their amazement at the time and energy which Prime Minister Churchill devoted to this procedure at all stages in the development of war policy. *On Active Service in Peace and War* shows Secretary of War Stimson doing the same.

President Roosevelt found the practice difficult, and a good many of his troubles came from this. Decisions made, or which seemed to have been made, on incomplete investigation or *ex parte* hearings, had to be modified or reversed, sometimes without everyone knowing that this had occurred. (Sir Winston tells us,

Thoughts about Thought in High Places

in *The Gathering Storm,* that his initial order on becoming the King's First Minister was that all decisions be put in writing. To many of us this innovation ranks in importance with the discovery of the wheel.)

The method and procedures I have mentioned are of the greatest help to the chief and to the staff, keeping in mind that cabinet members are both chiefs in their departments and staff officers to the chief of government. They provide a chief who can learn with the best means of doing so—information, carefully prepared; then a discussion of its meaning, conducted with spirit, criticism and relevance; and an indication of the course of action. They also give the chief timely opportunities to guide and stimulate the development of thought and action.

To the staff this practice is a constant demonstration both that their contribution is important and that it is fairly heard and considered. It is a stimulus to their best effort, a devastating arena for the poorly prepared or pedestrian mind, which soon disappears, and a method by which specialized experience and outlook, which must sacrifice breadth to depth, can adjust to the larger problem and purpose.

Even being present to see and hear the chief give his decision meets a fundamental, almost primitive, need of the staff. Confidence in leadership, loyalty to the processes of government, require first of all belief that commands put out in the name of the chief not only are, but authentically appear to be, his.

The curse of leadership has always been the majordomo, the chamberlain, the chief secretary, the favor-

ite—usually envied and disliked—who emerged from
the Presence with the Word. But whose word was it?
Did it have that authority behind it which demanded
obedience, or would a plot or a protest, a discreet leak
by "unimpeacable" sources to the press or to the Hill
—if that is not tautological—upset it? In a city where,
since the Gettysburg Address, few public men have
written their own utterances, one should not under-
estimate the importance of the chief's announcing, ex-
plaining, and, on occasion, discussing his decisions in
the presence of his staff.

One may predict with some assurance that any attempt to reorganize the highest echelons to give them
more time for thought will inevitably have two characteristics. It will cut the chief off from his principal
officers, and, in accordance with Parkinson's Law, it
will interpose new personnel, or "coordinating" staff,
between the chief and his principal officers.

The result will be that he will have to see just as
many people, but they will be the wrong people. His
reading may be reduced, but it will be predigested,
and both the protein of fact and the fermenting bac-
teria of conflict and criticism will be minimized in the
bland passage through an insulating special staff.

This has been the experience with the National Security Council. The NSC, in essence, is merely the
means for orderly and prepared meetings between the
President and a restricted group of his principal assistants charged with protecting the nation against danger
from abroad.

The problems which they can profitably discuss are

far easier to identify than to resolve. Cabinet officers and military officers prodded by their own assistants and by the President can identify them. To resolve them requires work within the departments, and between them, by the responsible officers at what is happily called the "working level," with constant reference to their chiefs and often discussion between them. If serious differences arise, as they often should, these are the stuff for Presidential thought and decision after argument and submission.

To interject into this refreshingly simple situation a new and separate staff for the NSC itself, as has been done, only complicates without improving. A few record keepers, agenda makers, prodders or gadflies, yes. But a separate staff cannot add knowledge, which remains in the departments, or responsible advice to the President, which is the duty and right of his cabinet secretaries. More bodies only clutter up a meeting and strain a flow of communication.

Organization—or reorganization in government— can often be a trap for the unwary. The relationships involved in the division of labor and responsibility as well as the channeling of communication and decision in any activity is far more subtle and complex than the little boxes which the graph drawers put on paper with their perpendicular and horizontal connecting lines. A good many years ago Chief Justice Taft said to a friend, "I have just been talking with So-and-So (using an eminent name) about what he calls the machinery of government"—then added, chuckling, "and, you know, he thinks it really is machinery."

Well, it is not that. The nature of an organization

and the relationships within it depend wholly upon what the people organized are supposed to do. I have a suspicion that the need for complexity in organization goes hand in hand with the extent to which those organized are dealing with physical things. In the field of thought, as such, its importance decreases, though no one would be foolish enough to suggest that it can be dispensed with. But where people are organized for thought, the simpler arrangements are kept, the better.

How, then, can the highest echelons increase their time for contemplation? There is only one answer. One cannot "make" more time—despite the colloquial phrase. One should not delegate contemplation. There remains disciplined and intelligent choice of how time is used.

Demands crowd insistently on a chief. Far more of them seem important than can be met. To weed out the time-wasters involves ruthlessness and some hurt feelings. It also involves some self-discipline. The importance of relaxation and quiet as inducements to contemplation has already been stressed. I would also stress that the use of all a chief's private time for competitive games, indoor and out, does not make for contemplation. A vast amount of reading is essential. So is relaxed, unhurried talk. So is quiet.

Obviously, ceremonies and the ceremonial side of politics—the endless palaver about the nonessential—offer fertile fields in which to harvest time. One could begin on Washington and Embassy society which, despite Allen Drury's entertaining novel of capital life, contribute nothing whatever in return for the time they take. The same is true of the public dinners—allegedly humorous, testimonial, or celebrant—put on by a hundred organizations, perennial or episodic. To put all of these invitations courteously to one side requires an appointments secretary with a Southern accent, a heart of ice, and a will of iron.

Then there is travel. Before World War II, tradition had it that the President never left the country. The occasion on which President Wilson broke the tradition did not encourage emulation. The same rule, though not so absolute, kept secretaries of state and other cabinet officers for the most part directing their departments.

Then, during and since the war, came the swing—and a most unfortunate one it was—to the opposite extreme. This is not the place for a review of conferences or meetings at the summit. I have done that elsewhere and concluded that there were only two successful ones in over 300 years—the Congresses of Münster and Osnabrück, which ended the Thirty Years' War, and the Congress of Vienna, which brought peace after the Napoleonic Wars.

Foreign Ministers' meetings have also become a menace. Former Secretary Brynes tells us that, of his 562 days' tenure in the State Department, 350 were spent at international meetings. Secretary Herter, as I write, has already clocked up 80 days out of 115 in office away from Washington. In large part this time was wasted, and that it would be was clearly foreseen.

On Public Service

Personal diplomacy at the top has largely become the substitution of improvisation for the sound and difficult domestic and foreign policies which would prevent us from getting into weak and exposed positions. Improvisation will not work, and all this traveling around depreciates the standing of those who, in any sensible system, should be the representatives of the Republic in communicating with foreign states. We are in a vicious circle in which the idea that only chiefs can talk to other chiefs keeps them rushing about so much that they do not have the time to devise and execute the policies which would make these frantic and repeated journeys unnecessary.

The time which the highest echelons need to think is not for brooding in isolated detachment; it is needed to devise the action to meet the exigencies of our times, to bring conviction of the need of that action to the Congress and people of the United States, and to explain it to the world. The hours which can be used for this lie all around them. At present, they are not being frugally used.

The President's Calendar: Two Typical Weeks

Friday, July 3
President Eisenhower is spending Friday at Camp David, Md. No appointments for him have been announced.

Thoughts about Thought in High Places

Monday, July 6

11:00 A.M.—Gordon Gray, special assistant on national security affairs.

11:30 A.M.—John H. Morrow, first United States Ambassador to Guinea, preparatory to departure for his post.

Tuesday, July 7

8:30 A.M.—Republican Congressional leaders.

11:00 A.M.—Gov. William Quinn of Hawaii and Interior Secretary Fred A. Seaton.

11:45 A.M.—Chairman John A. McCone of Atomic Energy Commission and Herbert Loper, Assistant to Secretary of Defense.

Wednesday, July 8

8:45 A.M.—Secretary of State Christian A. Herter.

9:00 A.M.—Rep. James V. Utt (R., Calif.) to discuss problems of the tuna industry.

10:30 A.M.—News conference.

11:30 A.M.—Harold T. Thomas, Auckland, New Zealand, president of Rotary International.

Thursday, July 9

9:00 A.M.—National Security Council.

11:00 A.M.—Secretary of State Christian A. Herter.

12:00 Noon—The three District of Columbia commissioners and representatives of the Virginia Corporation Commission and the Maryland Public Service Commission to present a report on mass transportation in the Washington area.

Friday, July 10

10:45 A.M.—Ned Cushing of Downs, Kan., chairman of the Young Republican National Federation, and the co-chairman, Mrs. David Frenald of Upper Montclair, N.J.

11:15 A.M.—A group of Junior Red Cross delegates prior to leaving on a European study tour.

11:30 A.M.—Rep. James Roosevelt (D., Calif.) and his three children Anna Eleanor, James Jr., and Michael.

(The President plans to remain at the White House over the weekend.)

Friday, July 24

President Eisenhower has no appointments scheduled for Friday. He plans to leave by helicopter about 11 A.M. to spend the weekend at his Gettysburg farm.

Monday, July 27

11:30 A.M.—Gen. Nathan F. Twining, Chairman of the Joint Chiefs of Staff.

12:00 Noon—Raymond J. Saulnier, Chairman of the Council of Economic Advisers.

Tuesday, July 28

8:30 A.M.—Congressional Republican leaders.

11:15 A.M.—Eric Johnston, chairman U.S. Committee for the Altantic Congress, to report on the Congress held in London last month.

Wednesday, July 29

7:30 A.M.—Breakfast with sixteen Republican members of Congress who belong to SOS Club.

Thoughts about Thought in High Places

10:30 A.M.—News conference.

11:15 A.M.—Directors of the Tennessee Valley Authority, Chairman Herbert D. Vogel and members A. R. Jones and Brooks Hays.

11:45 A.M.—Presents American Merchant Marine Achievement Award of the American Legion to representatives of the Pan Atlantic Steamship Corp. of Point Newark, N.J.

Thursday, July 30

8:30 A.M.—Sen. John Sherman Cooper (R., Ky.) and Reps. Howard H. Baker (R., Tenn.) and B. Carroll Reece (R., Tenn.) to discuss the TVA bill.

9:00 A.M.—National Security Council.

11:30 A.M.—Ernest B. Martin, Jacksonville, Fla., president, National Tire Dealers' Association, and W. W. Marsh, executive secretary, to invite President to association dinner here Sept. 14.

Friday, July 31

9:00 A.M.—Cabinet.

11:15 A.M.—Gov. LeRoy Collins of Florida, Reps. William C. Cramer (R., Fla.) and Robert L. F. Sikes (D., Fla.) and L. McHenry Jones, Pensacola, Fla., chairman of the Florida quadracentennial.

11:30 A.M.—Collins and other members of the executive committee of the Governors Conference, who recently visited the Soviet Union—Governors George D. Clyde of Utah, John E. Davis of North Dakota, Luther Hodges of North Carolina, Stephens L. R. McNichols of Colorado, Robert B. Meyner of New Jersey, Robert E. Smylie of Idaho, William G.

Stratton of Illinois and Cecil H. Underwood of West Virginia.

12:00 Noon—Members of the Brigham Young University Young Republican Club cited by the National Young Republicans organization as the outstanding club in the nation. The President expects to go to his Gettysburg, Pa., farm sometime in the afternoon.

Part Four ⋘

Illusion via Ideology

Morality, Moralism, and Diplomacy

We Americans are, for the most part, a pretty moral people, as these things go; certainly we set great store by morality. Our traditions are deeply rooted in the Puritan theocratic state of the seventeenth century and in the evangelical revival of the nineteenth. They are both Cromwellian and Wesleyan. It is true that we fall from grace often and far, not the least in our treatment of our fellowmen whose skins differ from the prevailing color, or whose religion differs from that locally accepted. This, and some of our other actions, lead people, viewing us from afar, to suspect us of hypocrisy. But they are wrong about this. We are only

Delivered at the University of Florida, Gainesville, Florida, February 20, 1958, and published substantially as given in *The Yale Review*, Summer 1958.

125

more like them than they had realized. We are all—as the Book of Common Prayer says—"miserable offenders," and our professions are beyond our practice; both we and our critics have erred and strayed from true ways "like lost sheep"; the remembrance of our misdoings should be "grievous unto us," though it seldom is.

All of this should not—and happily does not—make us any less determined to be guided by moral light; but it should lead us to take a modest view of our capacity to generate a beam pure and strong enough to be convincing to others.

Those who advocate what they refer to as a moral or idealistic foreign policy usually contrast this with what seems to them opportunism, or pure expediency. These terms are very slippery ones, and often elude a firm grasp. If we think about it, what is moral is characterized by what is excellent in conduct, and this is not explained much better by saying that excellence means what is right and proper, as against what is wrong, by established standards. At any rate morality would seem to be a branch of idealism, which affirms the pre-eminence of the product of mind and spirit in determining reality.

All of this seems a long way from what we usually hear discussed by people who call for moral or idealistic foreign policy. What they discuss seems more nearly moralism, the reduction of morals to maxims. These can easily be corrupted into slogans.

For instance, how seldom those who demand a moral policy appeal to the principles, the primacy of which is rarely denied, at least publicly—such principles as that to deal truthfully, honorably, and courageously is better than to practice duplicity, conspiracy, and treachery. Far more often the principles espoused are more complicated, and often closely related to the holder's most deep-seated prejudices and the limitations of his experience.

Let us think for a moment of a principle which is often put forward as a highly moral and idealistic one. This is that not only do communities which wish to break off existing political connections and become independent national states have a moral right to do so, but that a moral foreign policy on the part of the United States requires that we go to considerable lengths to help them, including the use of force, as President Wilson's Fourteen Points will recall to those who remember them. In that enumeration this principle was called the right of self-determination.

It was first applied against our enemies, whose resultant difficulties we could contemplate with commendable detachment, if not with enthusiasm. Its embodiment began with the dismemberment of the Austro-Hungarian and Ottoman empires. As one looks back upon the results in Eastern Europe and the Middle East, one has more difficulty in seeing the moral or ideal achievement than in recognizing the immediate, and, perhaps, irrevocable disaster.

Recently, however, to avoid complications, the principle has chiefly been invoked against our friends. Indeed, the more distant our relations with a state, the more restrained we appear to be in urging the moral

127

imperative of self-determination. With India, for instance, a particularly touchy, if not prickly friend, we are most reticent about mentioning the United Nations' call for a plebiscite in Kashmir, which India (for highly moral reasons, it insists) has alternately ignored and defied for the past eight years. Hungary is no longer what we lawyers call an active case. And need I speak of the Baltic states?

If this passion to free all men, everywhere, under all circumstances, and at once, is, indeed, a moral principle, it seems, as Mr. Louis Halle has pointed out, to partake more of the morality of John Brown than of Abraham Lincoln. Lincoln's moral attitude—excoriated as immorality by abolitionists and secessionists alike—disclosed what we might call a strategic, as against an ideological, approach to great and complicated problems. ". . . my paramount object in this struggle," he wrote to Horace Greeley on August 22, 1862 (almost as the armies locked in the crisis of the second Manassas) "is to save the Union, and is not either to save or destroy slavery. If I could save the Union without freeing any slave, I would do it; and if I could save it by freeing all the slaves, I would do it; and if I could do it by freeing some and leaving others alone, I would also do that. What I do about slavery and the colored race, I do because I believe it helps to save this Union; and what I forbear, I forbear because I do not believe it would help to save the Union. I shall do less whenever I shall believe what I am doing hurts the cause, and I shall do more whenever I shall believe doing more will help the cause. . . ."

Morality, Moralism, and Diplomacy

As I read these words and ponder them, I am comforted by the belief that Mr. Lincoln would have understood and approved stating principles in terms of their purpose and effect without characterizing them as moral or immoral.

To those who have any appreciation of the perils which surround us, of the lightning speed with which relative (indeed, absolute) positions can change, of the effect which popular attitudes, so easily and often unworthily stimulated, can have in forcing governments to foolish action or restraining them from wise action, a moralistic approach to foreign relations—and by this I mean one which attempts to apply the maxims or ideology of moral teaching—seems ill-adapted to the complexity of the task.

The moralistic-ideological approach to the conduct of foreign affairs consists in finding in one theme both a central evil, which is thought to dominate our time, and also the clue to its eradication. With the goal thus established and the weapon chosen, the ensuring operation can easily become a crusade. So to Senator [John F.] Kennedy, "the challenge of imperialism" was the "single most important test of American foreign policy." But President Eisenhower, in his State of the Union Message puts it differently. "Now, the threat to our safety and to the hope of a peaceful world, is simply stated. It is Communist imperialism." Note that the danger is not the power, military and otherwise, of the Soviet Union, which would be simpler still to understand, but "Communist imperialism." To Senator Joseph McCarthy the threat was Communists in

Illusion via Ideology

government. His crusade had the advantage of not tackling the difficult and dangerous task of countering a powerful and armed state, but only of browbeating frightened and defenseless minor employees of the government.

Among the more serious traps of this approach is the delusive simplicity it offers in choosing those whose purposes and efforts are helpful to our own, and those whose acts are hostile. If, for example, the central theme is that communism is the threat and evil, then those who most loudly assert their enmity to communism must, by this simple test, be our most assured co-workers in establishing an environment in which free societies can exist and flourish. So, in the past, both Hitler and Mussolini have been presented to us as dyed-in-the-wool anti-Communists, who not only made the trains run on time, but also represented the "wave of the future." So, also, more recently Generalissimo Franco has been hailed as a bulwark against communism.

Others are put off by Mr. Nehru. He does not seem to them wholly true-blue. He is critical of Western policy and apt to fall into enthusiastic applause at a good skit by Messrs. Bulganin and Khrushchev. Does he really belong to the team? The problem is, of course, quite different and wholly unrelated to considerations of this sort. Indeed, I have ventured to suggest that despite his "unusual gifts of causing annoyance, if Mr. Nehru did not exist, our greatest hope for India would lie in inventing him; for he, alone, seems to have a fair chance of holding India together while economic development lays a foundation for social and political stability."

The lesson is, of course, that, in determining those whom it is wise to support, the test is not what they say they oppose, but in the purpose and effect of what they are doing.

One could go on to point out the plethora of moralistic maxims which we have adopted. Forty years ago a principle was put forward as a sure foundation of the conduct of international relations which, since then, has had quite a vogue. This is the principle of "open covenants, openly arrived at." But today no less an authority than the Secretary General of the United Nations is not so sure.

> "Open agreements" represent the response to a sound demand [Mr. Hammarskjold said at Ohio University]. How and to what extent they should be "openly arrived at," on the other hand, is a principle which requires serious consideration in the light of the very aims which the public procedures are intended to serve.

And he added:

> The legislative process in the United Nations is not a substitute for diplomacy. It serves its purpose only when it helps diplomacy to arrive at agreements between the national states concerned. It is diplomacy, not speeches and votes, that continues to have the last word in the process of peace-making.

Illusion via Ideology

Again, toward the other end of the spectrum from the anti-Communist school are those who believe that the purpose and content of foreign policy must be to have "talks with the Russians." Where, when, by whom, about what, and to what effect seem comparatively unimportant. Here is a case, not of the end justifying the means, but apparently of the means justifying —or, at least, probably producing—a most unpredictable end.

Another approach, with which one can sympathize, if not approve, springs from the vast urge to do anything to lessen the horror of nuclear war and diminish its possibility. The terrible difficulty is that "anything" will not do this. The possibility of accomplishment by negotiation under present circumstances is small. The most promising courses are hard ones. Again, the best chance is not along lines of moralistic maxims, but along the Lincolnian approach—what I have called the strategic approach. If you ask me what I mean by a strategic approach, I could say a good deal but probably would not improve on Bret Harte's description of "Tennessee's Partner." "In fact, he was a grave man, with a steady application to practical detail which was unpleasant in a difficulty." The real task is to negotiate by action, sustained, wise, and disciplined action, by ourselves and our allies. Here lies, I believe, the best chance to convince the Russians that they cannot win by default, that in the end they must come to an understanding, and to assure that the understanding, whenever it comes—and it will not be soon—is one with which we, as well as they, can live.

Morality, Moralism, and Diplomacy

What I have said thus far is, first, that many of the moralistic maxims adapted to the conduct of foreign affairs are apt to reflect personal prejudice or sententious sentiment. Secondly, I have suggested that, even if these utterances were generally of a higher quality and more detached, one cannot find in ethics and aesthetics, alone, a complement of tools for dealing with the relations between states. Into these relationships enter factors govered by forces which operate in the physical rather than the metaphysical world. There also enters human conduct, which all too often is neither moral nor ethical nor controllable by exhortation. Those who, so rightly, admire the Gettysburg Address, should remember that it dedicated a field of action and was not a substitute for action. The conduct of foreign affairs must achieve its purpose by causes and effects of a varied and complicated nature upon a wide assortment of human, geographical, and physical material. From this activity moral factors are by no means absent.

As one probes further into the moral aspects of relations between states, additional causes for treading warily appear. A little reflection will convince us that the same conduct is not moral under all circumstances. Its moral propriety seems to depend, certainly in many cases, upon the relationship of those concerned with the conduct. For instance, parents have the moral right, indeed duty, to instill moral and religious ideas in their children and punish error. Ministers, priests, rabbis, and mullahs have much the same duties to their flocks, including that of correcting heresy, when they can make up their minds what it is.

Illusion via Ideology

But these same acts on the part of public officials in the United States would be both immoral and a denial of the fundamental rights of the citizen. Indeed, the attempt of both governmental and religious bodies to censor literature, painting, sculpture, the theater, and the movies, under the aegis of those alliterative adjectives, lewd and lascivious, seems to me intolerable. Parents, if they are any good, can shield their children from whatever they choose. The rest of us had better take our chances with mortal sin, rather than to have policemen, trained to handle traffic and arrest criminals, become judges of what art we may see or read. And it is just as bad when the local watch and ward society or church body tries to do the same thing.

So, acts, moral in one human relationship, may become quite the reverse in another. Generally speaking, morality often imposes upon those who exercise the powers of government standards of conduct quite different from what might seem right to them as private citizens. For instance, the moral, and indeed the legal, duty of a judge in bringing to bear upon a party before him the coercive power of the state is not to do "what he thinks is right," or by his decision to mold the kind of a society which seems to him to accord with divine will or high human aspiration. He has not been given this great power so that he might administer personal justice, even though his conscience be as clear as that of Harun al-Rashid or Henry II when they decided disputes by virtuous inspiration. Our courts are supposed to be courts of law; and whatever justice may be (I know of no satisfactory definition of it), it is to be achieved, as the phrase goes, "under law." It is our hope that the consciences of our judges will be guided, not by what they think is right, but what they believe the law requires them to decide, whether they like it or not.

So, too, what may be quite proper and moral for a private citizen—for instance, the pursuit of personal advantage, or the advantage of a group—often, and rightly, is condemned if done when he assumes legislative or executive powers in government. This distinction is not always perceived and has gotten many people into trouble. Recently a secretary of the air force resigned after conduct which is quite common and accepted in private life.

Even the individual, acting as such, may be under different standards depending on the capacity he may be required to, or wish, to assume. Take the supposed inalienable right to be ignorant and stupid, and to behave as such. Valid as this may be under many circumstances, it does not seem so inalienable when the individual acts as part of that indivisible sovereign, to the ultimate judgment of which all of us in this country must entrust our all.

Or take the point where the line should be drawn on selfishness, that offspring of the instinct of self-preservation. The standard is clearly different when an individual properly acts as an individual, competing with others, from what it should be when he acts as sovereign. For some years now the town on the banks of the Potomac where I live, and its northerly Maryland suburbs, have been trying to find some consensus on how to bring the expressway from the north into Washington. The only consensus so far developed is strong opposition to every route proposed. This has produced a cry of anguish from *The Washington Post.*

> The hearing in Maryland as well as that in the District brought out swarms of witnesses who were concerned about possible encroachments upon a backyard, a golf course, a piece of commercial property or plans for a real estate development. Are there no citizens or groups of citizens who can subordinate personal and neighborhood interests to the welfare of the community as a whole?

The editor did not stay for an answer probably because he knew it already, but he has put my point nicely.

To raise it in a larger and more controversial context, let me quote from a letter by Professor Sumner H. Slichter of Harvard, which appeared in *The New York Times* on February 9, 1958:

> The United States has never been able to develop a foreign trade policy that truly reflects the national interest. The making of our trade policy has always been taken over by various industries with political influence. As a result, our trade policy has been designed to advance the interests of favored industries to the detriment of the country as a whole.

Yet, I am sure that the National Association of Manufacturers would find nothing immoral in our past practices. The matter, as you see, has its complexities.

When we come, at last, to relations between states,

Morality, Moralism, and Diplomacy

rather than within a state, we find no consensus of opinion or monopoly of force to create and enforce standards. A great and powerful bloc of states rejects with cynical contempt almost all in which we believe; and says so quite frankly. The experience and condition of peoples of some other states differs so from our own that many of our most cherished beliefs—such, for instance, as the worth of the individual and all that flows from this—seem to them unreal and shadowy.

But, one may reply, at least some moral standards of right and wrong seem pretty well agreed. Surely, the opinion of the world has condemned the use and the threat of force by one state against another, as the United Nations Charter bears witness. Does this not give us firm ground on which to stand? Well, does it? Ever since the charter was signed, those whose interests are opposed to ours have used force, or the threat of it, whenever it seemed to them advisable and safe—in Greece, Czechoslovakia, Palestine, Berlin, Korea, Indochina, and Hungary. Both sides used it in regard to Suez. Is it moral to deny ourselves the use of force in all circumstances, when our adversaries employ it, under handy excuses, whenever it seems useful to tip the scales of power against every value we think of as moral and as making life worth living? It seems to me not only a bad bargain, but a stupid one. I would almost say an immoral one. For the very conception of morality seems to me to involve a duty to preserve values outside the contour of our own skins, and at the expense of forgoing much that is desired and pleasant, including—it may be—our own fortunes and lives.

This leads me to suggest an area in our foreign relations where guidance from what is excellent in conduct may more confidently be sought than in some others. This is in the methods by which foreign relations are conducted. There is pretty general agreement in some parts of the non-Communist world, as has been suggested, that it is better to act straightforwardly, candidly, honorably, and courageously than by means of duplicity, conspiracy, and treachery. For us to act on this principle will not reform our opponents, who will continue to use such methods whenever they suit their purposes. But it might do much to give them, as well as our own people, a much clearer idea of our intentions. This, in itself, would inspire confidence and increase stability. If this standard included a considerably greater insistence on truth than at present—not necessarily the whole truth, but, perhaps, nothing but the truth; not the conception of truth which enters the techniques of advertising, which is the gilding without the lily—the effect on policy might be great. For one thing, it would diminish the tendency to regard the art of diplomacy as the stratagem of going to the verge of war to accomplish a purpose.

I stress the application of this standard to the methods we use because I believe—although I am doubtless in the minority on this—that ends of action are not, for the most part, determined by ideals, but the other way around. It has been said that "Man . . . is born to act. To act is to affirm the worth of an end, and to persist in affirming the worth of an end is to make an ideal." And again, "Philosophy does not furnish motives, but it shows men that they are not fools for doing what they already want to do."

Morality, Moralism, and Diplomacy

Even though you find this doctrine unpalatable, you may still, as a practical matter, go with me to my conclusion. Not long ago, at another university, I was talking about the substance of desirable foreign policy. A student expressed the view that in stressing factors of power, of the capabilities of our own nation and others, I had left no place, as he put it, for moral or idealistic conceptions. I ventured to disagree, pointing out that the results of the policies I advocated would—and I knew of no others which could—stand a good chance of preserving not only our own nation, our allies, and I hoped, peace in the world, but also the whole civilization which had given us the values by which we lived, or tried to live.

Out of this Greco-Roman-Judaic civilization, with some of its roots in other cultures, had come the idea, and the often faltering recognition, of the worth of the individual, in whose mind and spirit all values must be tested. From this sprang freedom in all its forms—of mind and person and of communities of persons. From this civilization, too, had come unsurpassed teachings, in the dialogues of Socrates, the writings of Marcus Aurelius, and the Sermon on the Mount, of life committed to goodness and virtue. Among them is the teaching that strength is not itself a virtue—"blessed are the meek."

I pointed out to the young man that I found it hard to believe that to oppose a powerful and brutal state which was threatening the independence of others and, indeed, the existence of our civilization, was less admirable because it preserved our own nation as well. Nor did it seem to me less good to help peoples to improve their conditions because this was essential to keep the free world free and to strengthen it.

To be sure, policies of this sort required our forgoing other things. We had to pay for them with our taxes. This young man and others would have to give a part of that time in their lives, when they were eager to push on to the experience and responsibility of manhood, to military service, often irksome and wasteful.

But, surely, in all of this ideas played a vast part. And in the hierarchy of ideas which this policy produced, the highest and best which our prophets and teachers of the past had given us were at the top. What did he mean that this policy left no place for moral or idealistic conceptions?

But to return, in a closing word, to the methods we use. Here we can and should aim high. There should be no bullying, no advantage taken of the hardship of others to drive political bargains, no lying or boasting in our propaganda or our dealings with others, no sanctimonious lecturing of others on their faults, no consciousness of our own effortless righteousness, or the thanking of God that we are not as other men.

"Perhaps what we do is less important than how we do it. 'What one lives for may be uncertain,' writes Lord David Cecil of Conrad's view of life. 'How one lives is not. . . . Man should live nobly though he does not see any practical reason for it, simply because in the mysterious inexplicable mixture of beauty and ugliness, virtue and baseness in which he finds himself he must want to be on the side of the beautiful and the virtuous.' "

The Illusion of Disengagement

The other day I was re-reading Clarence
Day's wise and delightful book *This Simian World,*
and came across the paragraph remarking on what unpromising entrants in the struggle for supremacy on
this planet the lemurs might have seemed many millions of years ago. "Those frowzy, unlovely hordes of
apes and monkeys," he wrote, "were so completely
lacking in signs of kingship; they were so flighty, too,
in their ways, and had so little purpose, and so much
love for absurd and idle chatter, that they would have
struck us . . . as unlikely material. Such traits, we
should have reminded ourselves, persist. They are not
easily left behind, even after long stages; and they form
a terrible obstacle to all high advancement."

It does seem to be true that, in our day, only in a
sort of cyclical way do free societies retain an under-

Foreign Affairs, April, 1958.

141

standing of their own experience, and hold to the purposes which it has inspired. Is this because some echo
of those early traits still persists or because the inevitable hardening of the arteries of each generation brings
on some failure of memory, or for still other reasons?

Certainly moods change as memories, once fearful,
become dimmed, as new anxieties arise, and as present
exertions become increasingly distasteful. The bitter
teachings of 1914–1918, and the determination they
fired, had quite disappeared by 1938, to be replaced
by ideas of neutralism, withdrawal from conflict,
"America First." After these, in turn, were swept away
by the devastation of another world war and by a dis-
play of world leadership entailing vast national effort,
another twenty years has ended by bringing back the
old yearnings and errors under a new name. "Disengagement," it is called now; but it is the same futile—
and lethal—attempt to crawl back into the cocoon of
history. For us there is only one disengagement possible—the final one, the disengagement from life, which
is death.

Soon after we had awakened from the daze of World
War II, it became clear to us that our protected ado-
lescence as a great power was over. The empires which
had spawned us, whose capital had developed us, whose
balance of power had given us security, either disappeared in the two world wars or passed to more minor
roles. We were face to face with the responsibility of
adult national life in the most critical situation imagin-
able. A world which for a century had had an integral
life of sorts was split into three segments. One—the

The Illusion of Disengagement

Soviet-Communist segment, militarily unequalled, except in nuclear power in which it was weak, was held together by an ideological and economic system supported by force. Another—containing the vast populations of Asia, the Middle East, and North and West Africa was left in confusion and turmoil at the end of the war; and, in addition, either had newly gained national independence or was demanding it from rulers gravely weakened. To these people had come also expectations of an improving life to a degree never before imagined and, perhaps, unfulfillable.

The third segment was what was left of the old world order roughly Europe and the Western Hemisphere. The second and third segments had certain important common characteristics. They were not in the Soviet power system. But various and large parts of them could, under some conditions, be added to it.

In this situation, as it appeared not long after the end of World War II, the task of what has since come to be called the Atlantic Community, that is, the states of Western Europe and the Western Hemisphere, was to bring about and maintain with increasing strength and vitality a non-Communist world system. Within this system, not only the states mentioned, but those in the second segment as well, should, if the system was workable and working, be able to pursue their national ends in their own way.

This effort required, at the beginning, a great deal of reconstruction, particularly in Europe. The only state strong enough to furnish the leadership in this effort was the United States. Both its government and its people responded vigorously to the press of necessity. The steps which were taken are well known and need not be recalled here. The important thing is that they were successful in bringing about a common sense of purpose, certainly in Western Europe and the Western Hemisphere, and to a large extent were effective in giving opportunity to those nations in Asia and Africa which were just coming to the point where they were free to pursue their national destinies undirected from the outside.

Since the war, therefore, the foreign policy of the United States has become, by necessity, a positive and activist one. It has been one of attempting to draw together, through various groupings, that Western area which must be the center of a free and open world system, and of taking the leading part in providing it with military security, and with a developing economy in which trade could grow and industrial productivity could be developed, both in areas which were already industrially advanced and those which were at the threshold. At the same time it was an essential part of this policy to produce the maximum degree of cohesion throughout the whole non-Communist area, through political policies which would make for integration and strength rather than for exploitation.

Various aspects of this effort—the military, the economic, the political I have attempted to describe in some detail elsewhere. I have there pointed out the interdependence of the Western Hemisphere and Western Europe; how the power factors involved make it essential that this part of the world shall stand firmly

The Illusion of Disengagement

united; how, without the American connection, it is
impossible to maintain independent national life in
Western Europe; and how, without Western Europe,
the power factors would turn disastrously against the
United States.

Broadly speaking, these conceptions have for the
past decade or more had wide acceptance both in this
country and throughout the Western world. They
have been successful beyond the dream of those who
first advocated them. They are beginning to bear the
most valuable fruit.

Recently, efforts have been relaxed. Our military
security and much of our prestige resting upon it have
been impaired, though not so far that vigorous action
cannot make the necessary repair. But, throughout the
world, as I indicated at the beginning of this article,
voices are being raised to ask whether it is necessary
to continue facing the hazards of the military situation,
to continue bearing the expense of making vital and
progressive the economic life of the whole free world;
whether coexistence with the Communist system cannot be bought at a cheaper price and with less effort.
And so, when people are told, as they have been by
Mr. George Kennan, a man of the highest character
and reputation and justly entitled to a respectful hearing, that this is possible, his words have a powerful
impact.

Mr. Kennan's views are not new to him. They do not
spring from a fresh analysis of the current situation.
He has held and expressed these views for at least a
decade. The effect which they have had currently

makes us realize anew that the reception given to the expression of ideas depends upon the mood of the hearers. This reception may have little to do with the truth of the ideas expressed; it has a great deal to do with their power. Mr. Kennan has told people what they want to hear, though not because they want to hear it. What is it that he has said?

The ideas are almost as vague as the style is seductive. The thoughts are expressed as musings, wonderings, questionings, suggestions. But what comes out of it is about this: First, there is the idea of disengagement in Europe. By this is meant mutual withdrawal of American, British, and Canadian, as well as Russian, forces from somewhere. This somewhere first appears to be East and West Germany; then the "heart of Europe"; again, the Continent; and sometimes, from the general ethos of the discussion, it appears to be all overseas areas.

The second idea is the neutralization of Germany. The third is that there should be no nuclear weapons in Europe. And the fourth is that throughout Asia and Africa, in what are called the "uncommitted areas," there is little "to be done . . . except to relax"; that "It is perfectly natural that Russia . . . should have her place and her voice there too"; that "our generation in the West" has no "obligation vis-à-vis the underdeveloped parts of the world," and, anyway, there is no "absolute value attached to rapid economic development. Why all the urgency?" If any sound schemes for development are presented, we should support them, "when they arise"; but, only on

146

The Illusion of Disengagement

the condition that they tell us first "how you propose
to assure that if we give you this aid it will not be in-
terpreted among your people as a sign of weakness and
fear on our part, or of a desire to dominate you." If
Asian and African states should find in this grudging,
meager, and humiliating policy no opportunity to
push their economic development within the non-
Communist system, and should turn to Communist
methods and Communist help, we should accept their
action without concern and with good nature.

One sees at once that these conceptions are the very
opposite of those which the West has been following
for the past ten years or more. It is an assertion that
the struggle naught availeth; that it is dangerous, unwise, and unproductive. It is a withdrawal from positive and active leadership in the creation of a workable
system of states. It is a conception, blended of monas-
ticism and the diplomacy of earlier centuries, by which
the United States would artfully maneuver its way between and around forces without attempting to direct
or control them.

If we attempt to analyze these suggestions, the problems which they create promptly emerge. First, let us
consider the idea that something called disengagement
can be brought about by removing American, British,
Canadian, and Russian troops from some area in Europe. What disengagement does this bring about? Very
little, as one sees if one pauses to consider the realities.
Compare the confrontation which takes place between
the United States and the Soviet Union in Germany
with that which occurs along the DEW line—that sys-

tem of early warning stations which stretches from Alaska, across the Arctic regions and far out into the Atlantic. Here there are daily contacts on a thousand radarscopes, and doubtless the same is true on the other side of the screen. Some of these blips on the radar are actual aircraft; sometimes atmospheric conditions produce them. But they represent a contact which no action in Germany can disengage. There is confrontation in every part of the world where the area of the open and free world system may be reduced by Soviet military, economic, or political penetration. No action in Germany will produce disengagement here. The word is a mere conception, which confuses and does not represent any reality.

So, let us turn from it to consider something more capable of delineation. For instance, exactly what is the extent of the mutual withdrawal about which we are asked to negotiate? The answer to this question does not depend upon penetrating the vagueness of Mr. Kennan's language. For there can be little doubt, I believe, that, once a withdrawal begins, it will be complete, so far as United States, British, and Canadian troops are concerned. All the forces, foreign and domestic, will combine to bring this about. As the withdrawal makes the military position weaker, our forces will be less desired wherever they may remain. If withdrawal is represented as advantageous for Germans, it would seem equally advantageous to Frenchmen. Icelanders, Moroccans, Saudi Arabians, and the rest would quickly follow. And, once the idea caught hold, Americans would, of course, join in the general demand. The *New Statesman* shows us how the matter is now being presented to a small section of British opinion and how it could bemuse a still larger one in that country:

> Yet the missile agreement is one of the most extraordinary and complete surrenders of sovereignty ever to be made by the country for the exclusive benefit of another. For the missiles are not intended to defend Britain; on the contrary, they decisively increase its vulnerability. Their prime purpose is to reduce the likelihood of a Soviet ICBM onslaught on America during the crucial three-year period which must elapse before America possesses ICBMs herself. The sole beneficiary will be America.*

We should not deceive ourselves. After disengagement, we would soon find ourselves discussing complete withdrawal from all European areas and, very possibly, from bases in the Far East and Near East as well. Indeed, Mr. Khrushchev has twice served warning, once in Berlin in 1957 and again in January of 1958, that the sort of withdrawal which he is talking about is withdrawal from all overseas bases. This would cut the striking power of the free world by at least a half, and, perhaps, until our missile program accelerates, by much more.

We must think of what we purchase for this vast price. What would Russian withdrawal from Ger-

* "Britain's Suicide Pact," *New Statesman: The Week-end Review,* January 4, 1958, p. 1.

many or the heart of Europe amount to? Is it possible
to believe that the Soviet Government, whatever it may
say or whatever agreement it may sign, would, or could,
contemplate withdrawing its forces behind, say, the
River Bug, and keeping them there? And, by forces, I
mean effective Russian physical power, by whatever
name called. It is hard to see, after the events in Poland and Hungary, whatever the Russian Government
might wish, how it could possibly undertake so hazard-
ous a course. For, if its physical force were permanently
removed from Eastern Europe, who can believe that
even one of the Communist regimes would survive?
Therefore, wherever Soviet forces might be garrisoned,
the expectation and threat of their return must continue to be ever present (at most it would require
from twelve to eighteen hours) if Russia is to maintain the power which it has insisted upon as recently
as the Hungarian uprising.

At this point in our discussion we must examine the
conception of the neutralization of Germany; and then
bring together the consequences of withdrawal and
neutralization. It is necessary, we are told, that Germany should not be allowed to be free to choose its
own course after unification. It must accept limitations
upon its military forces and its military alignment. In
other words, its national life will be conducted under
far greater limitations than those in which other sovereign people live. The possibility that any such situation could endure seems to me quite fantastic.

Whatever Germans might initially think they would
be willing to do, there is no precedent in history for,

nor does there seem to me to be any possibility of, the successful insulation of a large and vital country situated, as Germany is, between two power systems and with ambitions and purposes of its own. Constant strain would undermine the sanctions of neutralization. The final result would be determined by the relative strength of the pressures from the two sides. As I have already suggested, the pressure would all be from the Russian side. For, there would be no power in Europe capable of opposing Russian will after the departure of the United States from the Continent and the acceptance of a broad missile-free area. Then, it would not be long, I fear, before there would be an accommodation of some sort or another between an abandoned Germany and the great power to the East. Under this accommodation, a sort of new Ribbentrop-Molotov agreement, the rest of the free world would be faced with what has twice been so intolerable as to provoke world war—the unification of the European land mass (this time the Eurasian land mass) under a power hostile to national independence and individual freedom.

But, without this withdrawal of forces and the neutralization of Germany, Mr. Kennan sees "little hope for any removal of the division of Germany at all nor, by the same token, of the removal of the division of Europe." Naturally enough, these words have found a strong echo in Germany. But it is a fading one, as Germans ponder the conditions which would flow from unification by withdrawal and neutralization, and see the end of the best hopes of the German people. Two weak states—East and West German jockeying for position in a sort of no-man's land, could raise the East-West "tensions" to a point compared to which anything we have yet experienced would seem mild indeed. In all this West Berlin would, of course, be the first victim. It would be a wholly inadequate judgment upon those whose naïveté and weakness produced this result that they should share the guilt of those Western politicians whose preaching of "liberation" encouraged the uprisings in East Berlin and Hungary, and, like them, should sit in supine impotence while more gallant men suffered. The best hope for German unification I shall mention shortly.

Turning to Eastern Europe, Mr. Kennan sees those countries, without the withdrawal of Russian troops, caught between the dilemma of constant revolutions, bloodily suppressed, and the acknowledgment of Soviet domination. This view seems to me founded on nothing but its assertion. I cannot for the life of me see how the movement toward a greater degree of national identity in Eastern Europe is furthered by removing from the Continent the only power capable of opposing the Soviet Union.

Nor do I see that the facts bear out Mr. Kennan's gloomy predictions. For instance, if the experience of 1956 had produced only the development in Poland or if the Hungarians had acted with as much restraint, it would have been plain to all that the attraction of the power of the West, of the possibilities which its system opens to all, was proving very strong indeed—stronger even than the secret police and Soviet occupation troops. The fact that in Hungary the reaction was pushed to the point where the Russians felt it necessary to suppress it with force proves only that it was handled unwisely.

So, as we think about the matter, we must wonder whether there is anything we can purchase "one-half so precious as the goods" we sell. We are told not to worry about this; that, even though it seems quite unlikely that the Russians would carry out any withdrawal, nevertheless, it is good propaganda to make the offer and cause them to refuse it. This seems to me profoundly false. In the first place, it treats international negotiations as though all the figures on the chessboard were made of wood or ivory; whereas, in fact, we are dealing with living people, subject to all the emotions of mankind. If I were a European and had to live through two or three years of American negotiations about withdrawing from the Continent, I think that very early in the game I would discount America's remaining and would prepare to face a new situation. Furthermore, to believe that the Russians can be put in the position of refusing to evacuate Europe underrates their skill in negotiation. They would simply, as they have already done, continue to raise the price. And it would be we and not they who would do the refusing.

The evils of a timid and defeatist policy of retreat are far deeper than its ineptness as a move in the propaganda battle. It would abandon the efforts of a decade, which are bringing closer to realization the hopes of Western Europe, of Germany, and of Eastern Europe

153

as well. From the low point of 1946–1947 the economic, social and political health and strength of Western Europe—of which West Germany has become an integral and vital part—have grown greatly. Their pull on Eastern Europe continues to mount. To continue this the American connection is essential. The success of the movement toward unity in the west of Europe is no longer in doubt. Only the rate of progress is undecided. The Coal and Steel Community, Euratom, the Common Market have been accepted. A common currency and political community are on the way.

All of this is threatened by the call to retreat. It will not do to say that a united Germany, made militarily impotent and neutralized, can play an effective part in bringing to fruition a united and vigorous European community. The slightest puff of reality blows this wishful fancy away. The jockeyings and tensions of the two parts of Germany, the unopposable threat of Russian power, the bribes which can be dangled before Germany by the Soviet Union in the form of boundary rectifications and economic opportunities— these alone are enough to put an end to hope of a united and strong Europe, invigorated by Germany.

For those who believe that Eastern Europe would welcome American and Russian troop withdrawls as the beginning of liberation, I suggest a quiet sampling of candid Polish opinion. I venture to predict that what they would find is a horror at being abandoned by the West and left between the Soviet Union and a Germany similarly abandoned, to which the offer of another partition of Poland might be irresistible.

But, if one looks at the other side of the medal, what a different face it bears! A strong, united Europe could have the men and the resources—along with British and United States contingents—to deal by conventional forces with invasion by conventional forces, particularly as the Eastern European satellites are becoming a danger, and not an asset, to Soviet military power. This, if pressed, gives real mutuality of benefit to a negotiated reduction in forces. It makes possible, too, a time when nuclear forces would no longer have to be relied on as a substitute for conventional forces, and with it a real opportunity to negotiate this threat further and further into the background.

Finally, a thriving Western Europe would continue its irresistible pull upon East Germany and Eastern Europe. This would, in turn, have its effect upon the demands of the Russian people on their government. With a rise in the standards of living in the Soviet Union, and as some broader participation in the direction of affairs was made essential by their very magnitude and complexity, the Russian need for the forced communization and iron control of Eastern Europe would diminish. Then negotiations looking toward a united Germany, under honorable and healing conditions, and toward the return of real national identity to the countries of Eastern Europe, while preserving also the interests of the Russian people in their own security and welfare, could for the first time be meaningful and show the buds of hope. This has been the goal of Western policy for the past decade.

Illusion via Ideology

It would be self-delusion to close our eyes to the difficulties which lie before us along this road. Some we have created ourselves. Our military strategy, with its sole reliance on massive retaliation, and a budgetary policy which has neglected even that, have caused us a loss of relative military power and of prestige. Some of our political policies have weakened our alliances. Our allies, too, are having their troubles. In what are perhaps the two closest of them, we could wish (as they undoubtedly do, too) that both the present and the immediate future held greater promise for the development of strength and popular attitudes more attuned to reality. We all share together the common problem of devising a military policy for NATO which will avoid making the proposed defense seem as fearsome as the potential enemy's threat, and which will be a real deterrent because it is a credible one.

I have suggested elsewhere that this is possible. Briefly, the way is to create a situation in fact which equals the political purpose of the North Atlantic Treaty—that is, a situation where in order for the Soviet Union to attack, or coerce Europe, it would have to attack, or coerce, the United States as well. This, if we all use a fair degree of intelligence about our defenses, the Soviet Union could be deterred from doing. What is required is a short-range effort which does not preclude a sustained effort toward a wiser long-range goal. The short-range effort would be to provide NATO with such effective nuclear power that the Soviet Union could not have its way without destroying that power; and an attempt to destroy it would be impractical apart from a simultaneous attempt to disable the United States, which could be made too dangerous. The longer-range purpose would be to develop adequate conventional forces in Europe, with British and American participation, to make mutually desirable a real reduction and equalization of both Soviet and NATO forces and a controlled elimination of nuclear material for military use.

I quite understand that all of this is difficult. But I believe also that "the mode by which the inevitable comes to pass is effort."

Finally, Mr. Kennan's discussion of the uncommitted countries of Asia and Africa seems to me to disclose a complete lack of understanding of the forces which are at work there. In the first place, he would like to tell them, as Thoreau would have done, that the whole march of industrial civilization since the beginning of the nineteenth century has been a mistake; that they must be patient about increasing their standard of living; that they must curb the mad rate at which they reproduce; that we have no sense of guilt or obligation to them because we are in a position to help their economic development as our own was helped. But when they have any sound plans, we will consider them on terms which they cannot accept. This means that we find nothing to our interest in their industrialization; and that they are in reality ward heelers who threaten one political side with desertion to the other unless they receive a handout or a sinecure.

Nothing could be further from the truth. These

governments are faced with a demand, just as are the government of the United States and the government of the Soviet Union, that conditions shall exist under which a rising standard of living is possible. The conditions in these countries vary from those which are still deep in an agricultural stage to those which have begun industrialization and are ready, once capital is available, to push it speedily forward. Governments cannot stay in power unless they respond to the demands of those who will keep them there. Even the oligarchs in the Kremlin are under pressure, which they cannot altogether refuse, to expand the standard of living in Russia.

There are two ways in which the governments of the undeveloped countries can bring about conditions which their peoples demand. Both of these involve acquiring capital, but under very different conditions. One involves the adoption of totalitarian authority, a temporary depression of the standard of living, forced savings, and industrial equipment from Russia, paid for by the export of raw materials. The other involves the maintenance, and perhaps a steady expansion, of the standard of living, the maintenance of systems of government in which there is a considerable area of freedom, the import of capital from Western Europe and North America, and the repayment of these loans over a considerable period of time by participation in the expanding trade of an open economic system. To say that economic development has nothing whatever to do with political alignment is a fallacy of the gravest sort. It is, of course, true that economic aid cannot force, cannot ensure, a political alignment from any country. But it is certain that, without it, a different alignment will take place.

May I conclude by repeating that the new isolationism which we have been discussing, and the reception it has received, is gravely disturbing, not only because it is utterly fallacious, but because the harder course which it calls on us to forego has been so successful. If one compares the non-Communist segments of the world today with what they were twelve years ago, one sees enormous progress. If one compares, as we have tried to do here, the pull of a vigorous free system, held together by the joint efforts of at least some of its members to provide military security, economic power and political leadership, one sees how strong it is and what effect it has had. If one considers the changes which have already occurred within the Soviet Union, one can see the time approaching when adjustments in Eastern Europe are possible, when military forces can be reduced, and when the menace of nuclear destruction will be greatly diminished, if not removed. Surely, there are dangers, and great dangers, but with good sense we can live through these. We will not make them less by weakening ourselves, destroying the confidence of our allies, and refusing to help those people who are willing to work to some extent, at least within the system which we and our allies, together, have created and can make ever more vigorous and appealing.

The American Image
Will Take Care of Itself

Nothing so fascinates and frustrates Americans as foreign affairs. Councils, forums and institutes on the subject draw young and old alike, as did missionary societies and Chautauquas a half-century ago. The reason for fascination with a world pressing in on us, as does ours today, is obvious. The reason for frustration is the intractability of the foreigner, his insensitivity to American views. But not a little is subjective, too: An American is apt to stare like Narcissus at his image in the pool of what he believes to be world opinion, until he pines away; or else, he makes himself over into the image he would like to see, only to have his shrewder self tell him that he looks a fool.

Each would shape his image a little differently, but

The New York Times Magazine, February 28, 1965.

the main ingredients would include a bit of Thomas Jefferson, Alexander the Great, the Statue of Liberty, Henry Ford and the Ford Foundation. We catch this Narcissus psychosis from Madison Avenue, but the reason for the mask lies deeper. "Man's crude spontaneous self," Lord David Cecil explains, is "merely a bundle of impulses without value or significance: he should therefore choose and assume a mask that represents his personal ideal, his conceptions of what, taking account of his capacities and limitations, he should aspire to be. Thus he will endow his life with beauty and meaning: if he retains the mask and consistently acts in character with it, he may even ultimately assimilate his nature to it, become substantially the personality he presents to the outer world."

To be susceptible to Narcissus-image worry, a society must value more highly than its own some outside opinion of itself—in other words, feel insecure. Some don't, and some do. For a time our ancestors worried about what was thought about them in heaven and tried to adapt their image accordingly. But we don't worry about that any more. Some of us believe that we are on the side of the angels, or vice versa; others that there aren't any. When we worry, we worry about foreigners—and how we worry!

It has always been this way; and it has always got us down. We started out as colonials, or worse, and being treated as such—Geroge III set the fashion. Old Ben Franklin and John Adams resented it when they got to London. But not even Charles James Fox and Edmund Burke could get the British to lower their eye-

161

brows; and the French let us into their houses by the front door only because they knew it would annoy the British.

Even when we thought, and with justice, that we were getting to be somebody, Mr. Charles Dickens told us just what sort of a somebody it was. For over a century we have paid foreign lecturers millions to cultivate our inferiority complex. We have learned to double our tips when English butlers eyed them coldly, and to believe that every glance directed at us, whether from patrons of sidewalk cafes along the Champs-Elysées or peasants up to their knees in Asian paddy fields, was double-sighted along a nose as elegant and elevated as General de Gaulle's.

What is more, we are even led to worry not only about the impression we make but about the truth of what we have actually done. For instance, we had believed that last autumn we joined the Belgians for purely humanitarian reasons to save the lives of unfortunate doctors, teachers, priests, and nuns in the Congo, whose only offense had been the simple and admirable desire to minister to its people. But after the debate in the United Nations some of the more advanced cases of reflection-worry began to see the operations as imperialist-capitalist-monopolist interference in the internal affairs of a sensitive and innocent people engaged only in their normal preparations for Thanksgiving.

At any event, a country half slave—or all slave—to foreign criticism cannot stand, except as a mental institution. We cannot gird ourselves for the war against poverty or in Vietnam until we exorcise image worship. The Greeks have given us the prescription; psychiatry, the method. "Know thyself," said Socrates. Today we say the same thing a little differently, "Be yourself." But how? The symbol of the Greek command was a mirror. But our mirror reflects not ourselves, rather the masks we wear in our pathetic eagerness to please others. So turn from the mirror, like the Lady of Shalott, and look at the world directly. The mirror will not crack from end to end. It exists only in our minds. No curse will come upon us, for we shall have exorcised the curse.

Psychiatry exorcises by exhuming fears, from the darkness in which troubled minds have buried them, for candid examination in the light of consciousness. So, we may ask, what is this world opinion which so deeply impresses us and which we are so eager to impress? How is it formed and on what grounds? Who holds it? Who discovers and reports it? When we answer these questions, we shall be free once again.

No one, I suppose, imagines that world opinion is discovered by pollsters going from door to door in Lancashire, Provence and Hesse asking, "Do you approve of the multilateral force?" Or in Indonesia, soliciting views on whether Malaysia is good or bad for Indonesian exports; or in India, inquiring about agreement or disagreement with American policy on settlement of the Kashmir dispute; or in Ghana, about the American demand that our sovereign equals in the United Nations pay up or quit voting. Honest answers to these questions would be unanimous "don't knows."

Of course, protests could be arranged in all these

Illusion via Ideology

disparate places against any positive American action. People could be induced to march and, perhaps, sit in driveways in Europe, and to march, break windows and even burn American Information Libraries elsewhere. But these protests would not represent local popular opinion; they would represent instigation and organization.

World opinion simply does not exist on the matters which concern us. Not because people do not know the facts—facts are not necessary to form opinion—but because they do not know that the issues exist. Opinion, like yeast, is produced by fermentation from other opinion. When a man, after reading a pundit's column at breakfast, holds forth himself at lunch, he does not know any more about the subject than he did before, but he has an opinion. A bit of the pundit's yeast has fermented within him; and since often there was little else within him to be fermented, the result is likely to be hot air.

But I am getting ahead of my story. Granted that pundits, by written and spoken word, disseminate a nonexistent world opinion, where do they get it, and what do they give for it? They give the means and often the assurance of dissemination. World opinion they get from one another, from lesser disseminators, demeaningly called "the working press"—and as the result of an annual "fact-finding" tour. On this tour they visit the sources of opinion open to the working press, which in most of the world is the government, or those kept by the government. If they are pundits of prestige, they may have a private interview with (until recently) Mr. Khrushchev or General de Gaulle.

Governments produce local opinion, chiefly for export, on subjects which are deemed suitable for opinion. It may be designed to please or to frighten, to assure loyalty or threaten defection; or the source may spar for time, in which case opinion is said to be "vacillating." The working press meets working businessmen, who have drunk from the same spring. Over different drinks they confirm one another's impressions; and someone gives the word to the CIA. Occasionally one of our own ambassadors, and not always a political appointee, takes to excessive consumption of local source material and becomes, himself, a producer of world opinion.

In the more sophisticated countries sources of opinion may be controlled by antigovernment as well as government groups; and there is a possibility, though not a great one, that a fraction may be independent.

The London and Paris opinion factories reward with appreciated attentions those who play the game with them. At small and exquisite luncheons in the Quai d'Orsay leaks, true or speculative, are sprung; a bit of racy gossip dropped about a colleague; a good story told of a fellow countryman's gaucherie at the last meeting of NATO ministers, and so on. In London distribution is aided by political society. It is rather less subtle, but quite as effective. In Rome even the working press is too confused to devise a pattern of opinion from the minuet danced by Christian Democrats of varying shades, Communists, Socialists (Saragat and Nenni), Liberals, Neo-Fascists and Monarchists.

If one would like to see opinion factories at work, an interesting exhibit centers in the United Nations Building on the East River, at the time of the Assembly's general debate, and spreads out of meeting rooms into lobbies, hotels, restaurants and bars all over New York. These factories vary from chromium-plated noiseless ones, where all is automation and the human hand never appears, to little one-room jobs with two girls, a boy and a mimeograph. Often, too, the whole process is run off in one day as a sort of classroom demonstration, from the contrived incident abroad to the report, "African Opinion Condemns U. S." in the New York newspapers.

But usually, of course, the span between production and publication of opinion is longer. First, reports as numerous as lumps in a cargo of metal ore are shipped home, then smelted into opinion ingots. Then the ingots must be cast, rolled, bent, twisted and hammered into world opinion, or area—usually large area—opinion. "Europe Cool to MLF"; "Latin America Disillusioned on Alliance"; "Africa Rejects Tshombe," and so on.

Out of such stuff is formed the body of folklore which Americans accept as World Opinion—world judgments on what they are, what they do and why they do it. Not by any stretch of the imagination could the folklore represent the opinions of people. Its very sources, manner of collection, and preparation for the market preclude that. It may, and often does, give a good idea of what the government of a country and occasionally the opposition would like to have believed was the opinion of its people. But, as to their actual opinions, if on these subjects more than a few have any, the folklore purveyed gives not a clue.

The effect and use of this artificial folklore is curious too; and a little unexpected. The immediate result is to convince those who produce it that it is the genuine article, and to furnish ammuntion for controversialists whose positions have already been taken for quite different reasons. Upon the customers, the American people, the effect is very gradual and very general. In a way it is not unlike that of the automobile. The automobile kills a lot of people, but doesn't frighten anyone. It has made the whole population mobile, but hasn't led anyone to go to any particular place.

So it is with this matter of world opinion. It plays overtime upon our inferiority complexes. We are setups for the caricatures of the Ugly American, of the stupid diplomat, the contemptuous, grasping, wily foreigner taking our money at the other end of the rat hole down which we fatuously pour it, or our obtuseness in getting into wars we should have stayed out of, and getting out of wars we should have stayed in and enlarged. Sometimes when we worry about a task which is hard, or unrewarding, or complicated, or all three, it is tempting to listen to foreign sirens, even if spurious ones, telling us to rest in the shade and eat the lotus.

The short of the matter is that world opinion,

Illusion via Ideology

whether thought of as fairy light or hobgoblin, to be-
guile or to frighten, is, like them, pure fancy—no more
substantial a ghost than the banging of a shutter, or
the wind in the chimney. It is like that elusive man in
the verse:

> *As I was going up the stair,*
> *I met a man who wasn't there.*
> *He wasn't there again today.*
> *I wish to God he'd go away!*

The American Image, too, will take care of itself if
we get on with what we have to do in, as our great-
great-grandfathers would have said, the station to
which it has pleased God to have called us, or less ele-
gantly, in the spot we're in. Old Mark Twain summed
it up pretty well. "Always do right," he said. "This
will gratify some pople, and astonish the rest."

Part Five ⋘

The Vast
External Realm

Southern Africa

There is a deep misunderstanding in the United States about our relations with what the Supreme Court has called "the vast external realm." This phrase is particularly poignant. It brings home to us clearly that foreign relations deal with the world outside of any direct influence which we can bring to bear. Our writ does not run in the vast realm. Our influence is minimal. Only if we use our tremendous force can we give sure effect to our will. Even then, as we have learned perhaps to our regret, we cannot exercise our will for long.

In Vietnam, we are going through this experience now. Both in Japan and in Germany, we learned the lesson very shortly after the last war.

Statement made before the Subcommittee on Africa of the House Committee on Foreign Affairs, Washington, D. C., November 19, 1969.

The Vast External Realm

Dean Inge observed that a man may build a throne from bayonets but then cannot sit upon it. We can do almost anything with force; as long as we are trying to overcome opposing force. Once that opposing force has been overcome, one must go back to the elemental rules and necessities involved in dealing with the external realm. One must then try to influence people, either by persuasion or by such other noncoercive means as one can bring to bear.

Force does not work, unless one is willing to be as ruthless as the Russians have been in Czechoslovakia. When they found that state moving away from their ideological conceptions, they moved the army in. They took over the whole country. In effect they govern it.

In dealing with the vast external realm, one must measure one's power, one must measure one's influence and above all, one must measure one's vital interests.

By painful experience over the centuries there has come an understanding that each state should respect the autonomy, with respect to internal affairs, of every other state existing in the vast realm external to its own boundaries. That precept is basic to whatever hope there is for peace and order in the world. That it is occasionally violated is no reproach to its validity.

I think this lesson came home to people in the Western world with great force in the seventeenth century. The wars of religion reduced the population of Europe by about one-third—probably more destruction than the Black Death ever accomplished. For thirty years, multitudes died of hunger, died violent deaths, and expired under every form of misery that one man could inflict upon another. At the end of that period, it became the stated rule of international relations in Europe that the internal affairs of a country were no proper concern of other governments.

What is properly of concern to us is any impingement of another country upon our interests. Such an impingement may occur when another state makes war on us, that would be the most violent example. It may come when another interferes with our trade, or with our investments, with our freedom of movement, or with other things which we consider to be vital. These are proper matters for interest by the United States.

We have been learning this lesson for ourselves painfully, in regard to Latin America. At one time, Americans thought it was proper and necessary to intervene with arms in Latin America, especially in the Caribbean, whenever there was a default on servicing a debt, or whenever authority faltered or disorder became rampant. Then we discovered that this did not work. The moment the marines were withdrawn matters reverted to where they had started. Our actions incurred bitter enmities for us in Latin America. If Latin America is united on one thing, it is on the doctrine that there shall be no interference by the "Colossus of the North."

I believe this concept to be the primary rule of international relations.

This rule has been written into the Charter of the United Nations in a provision, in paragraph 7 of article 2, that nothing in the charter shall be construed in any way to permit interference by that organization in the internal affairs of any state.

Of course, if a state makes war, and if the United Nations or governments acting under United Nations authorization intervene in that war to restore peace, it may be necessary to interfere with the state's internal affairs. Presumably the state will have been conquered. Those who have conquered it must run it until they turn it back to its own government. This, by the way, they must do fairly promptly, as we found out both in Germany and in Japan.

We should not intervene for what are called moral reasons in the internal affairs of another country. Moral reasons for interfering are merely a cover for self-indulgent hypocrisy.

Consider the case of Rhodesia. We will not fight the country. We will not take it over. We will not assume responsibility for governing it. We will try, however, to cause it so much harm that it will capitulate and do our bidding. Without having caused ourselves much inconvenience or incurred costs and risks, we can then go to bed happily at night, saying, in a mood of self-congratulation: "We have been very moral. We have made those wretched people suffer because they do not do what the Warren court would like them to do by applying the idea of one man, one vote."

This way of acting, I believe, is immoral and wrong.

The moral doctrine, the correct doctrine, is that we should not interfere in the internal affairs of another state.

174

Now let me move to economic sanctions. The chairman has stated, and stated quite correctly, that economic sanctions against Rhodesia have not worked. Likewise, restrictions against Portugal and South Africa with respect to trade in arms have not worked.

I shall add that such undertakings will not work. They are futile. They are ill advised.

This is a matter with which I have had a good deal of experience myself, and I would like to draw on that briefly.

During the war against the Axis I represented the State Department in all the activities of the government in connection with economic warfare. It was particularly interesting, and it is relevant to this discussion, that in our dealings with the European neutrals, in our efforts to prevent them from supplying Germany with war materials, we brought to bear upon them the full effect of our economic power, so far as we were able to exercise that power from the sea.

We had complete, absolutely complete, control of the sea. The blockade which we established was pervasive. No vessel could move one mile on the sea without a navicert from the British and American governments. No one could buy anything anywhere in the world, much less transport it to Europe, without permission from the British and us.

We brought this vast power to bear in three particular points. One was Sweden. Another was the Iberian Peninsula—Spain and Portugal. The third was Switzerland.

All of those countries were dealing importantly

with Germany—very importantly indeed. We brought our pressure to bear on them in two ways. As one way, we offered to buy, and did buy, everything that they could produce and wanted to sell abroad. Two purposes guided this effort.

One purpose was to prevent these things from getting to Germany. The other purpose was to make their cost to Germany excessive insofar as Germany could get hold of them. The other thing we did was to prevent anything from going to these countries unless their governments would agree to reduce their exports to Germany to the very minimum.

In a book which I recently published, called *Present at the Creation*, I review, on page 62, the success or failure of these operations over the entire course of the war, a matter with which I was intimately familiar, both as a member of the original Board of Economic Warfare and subsequently, until the end of the war, as the State Department's respresentative on various successors to that board.

The conclusion I come to is that, although this effort cost Germany a good deal, our preclusive purchases, our blockade policies, and our economic restrictions really accomplished almost nothing.

So far as Sweden was concerned, we materially reduced Swedish exports of ball bearings, which were the most important exports that Sweden made to Germany, about six months before our military forces stopped them altogether. In other words the entire pressure from the sea on Sweden, which was highly vulnerable to pressure from the sea, hastened trouble for German production, with respect to the key item, by about six months over the total interruption of those by the armies of the United States. German troops moved through Sweden virtually to the end, despite our efforts to press with economic restrictions.

In regard to Switzerland, our effort did not make any difference at all. Switzerland reduced its transport to Germany only after our military operations blocked communications.

In regard to economic restrictions on the Iberian Peninsula, we had some differences with our British ally. We favored and exercised a total prohibition of imports. Thereby we made no impression on either the Spanish or the Portuguese.

So I point out to you that, in the light of experience, economic sanctions are delusory. The longer they are continued, the more irritation is caused, and the more heavily the burden of them falls where you do not wish it to fall.

In Rhodesia, the burden of sanctions falls most heavily on the black population, among whom considerable unemployoment has been caused.

I come back to something that I briefly touched on a moment ago. If one is going to interfere in the internal affairs of a country by economic sanctions, not only is one going to be unsuccessful, but also one is doing something basically wrong, if not indeed wicked. That is to say, one engages in an attempt to foment civil disturbance, uprisings, revolution, and violence within a friendly state.

One may properly attempt such things against enemies in the course of a war. We tried to do this in Europe, and we tried to do it in Japan—in both places unsuccessfully—during the war of a quarter century ago. To seek such results within friendly states is another matter entirely. It is in my judgment indefensible.

Let me speak now briefly about the importance of southern Africa, all of southern Africa, to the United States.

An important aspect, yet the one I regard as the least important of the three, concerns our economic interest in all of southern Africa. There are great mineral deposits in which there are various substantial American investments. They are a proper source of interest. If we proceed with such hostility as we are now proceeding with, the course must inevitably lead to the loss of those investments.

Such a result, I should think, would be manifestly contrary to the national interest. This aspect is not, however, as important as the other two.

With the movement of the Russian Navy into the Eastern Mediterranean and into the Indian Ocean, and with the closing of the Suez Canal, the route around the Cape becomes of great importance not only to the United States but indeed to the world. Cargoes which formerly moved through the Suez Canal, particularly oil cargoes, now must go around the Cape. We are building, and other nations are building, tankers so large that they could not use the Suez Canal even if it should be reopened. The Suez Canal is turning out to be a nineteenth century venture, whose usefulness and significance are diminishing in our time. Henceforth the main maritime route will be around the Cape of Good Hope. That being so, we must take care that the ports there shall be in friendly hands and that they shall be open to use by shipping of the Western world in general. The ports not only of South Africa, at the tip of the Cape, but also of Portuguese Africa, along the east and the west coasts, are of great importance to us. For those ports ever to fall into unfriendly hands would be most unfortunate.

The greatest of our interests in southern Africa is connected with our deep concern for the stability and development of all Africa. An essential element of the best hope for that course in sub-Saharan Africa concerns the role of Portuguese Africa, South Africa, and Rhodesia. Here are resourceful and sound developing economic communities. They are technically competent. They have capital. The governments concerned are willing and able to aid their black neighbors in a sort of sub-Saharan African point four program.

The intiative for this program is spearheaded by the very able Foreign Minister of South Africa, Mr. Hilgard Muller, with whom I have talked on many occasions about this program. Indeed, a difference about this program is the cause of the recent division in the Nationalist Party in South Africa. The traditional members believe that this program constitutes a departure from the precepts of apartheid. They therefore oppose it and are challenging Prime Minister Vorster's government.

Prime Minister Vorster and Mr. Muller believe

that the interest of everyone in southern Africa will be furthered by the progress and development of South Africa's black neighbors, of whom Malawi is the most cooperative.

If and when sanctions are given up, Zambia will fall in line. Other British Commonwealth black republics will probably go along. I believe very soon some of the other black nations will do likewise.

The standard of living among some of the blacks in southern Africa is higher than it is for many areas of black Africa. The level of livelihood can be pushed higher yet. Everybody will benefit from such developments. The South Africans will benefit. The Portuguese will benefit. The Rhodesians will benefit. All the black countries will benefit. The world will benefit.

Nobody benefits from violence and conflict as found in Nigeria and Biafra. These are horrible reversions to primitive tribalism. If, in contrast, the countries in southern Africa can lead in development and in stability, they will be performing a great service to the world. We ought to do everything we can to further such a development rather than abetting the opposite course.

Now let me have a more immediate look at the three countries, and then I will end by centering on Rhodesia.

I have already spoken briefly about Portuguese Africa. Several other aspects should be kept in mind. As one, the Portuguese were in Africa before Columbus discovered the Western world. This is no Johnnycome-lately operation. This is no nineteenth century nouveau-riche attempt to establish spheres of influence in Africa. This establishment goes back for centuries.

We can see some interesting comparisons with our own history in North America. For instance, Angola and Mozambique are largely populated by Africans. North America is not nearly populated by Indians. We are now, in anxiety, striving to civilize the Indians after a phase approaching extermination. We have put them on reservations. We have expropriated their property, and sometimes, I feel we ought to give a good deal of it back to them with gain to ourselves. That thought, however, may reflect a personal prejudice. I think the Indians really sold a gold brick when they traded away Manhattan Island.

In Portuguese Africa, Africans constitute the vast majority, are happy, and get along as well as anywhere in Africa.

A recent article in the *London Times* observed: "Unrest in Black Africa is not a product of black Africans, but is the product of those who have been taken abroad, educated according to Western standards, and reintroduced into a tribal society for which they are no longer suited." I offer this as an observation of fact.

Portuguese Africa is undergoing rapid change. The Portuguese understand realistically that Portugal is a small and weak state. It cannot withstand great external pressure. Therefore, the Portuguese are Africanizing the administration of both Angola and Mozambique as rapidly as they can. This reflects a hope of maintaining, as part of Portugal, areas which they regard as part of Portugal as much as we regard Hawaii or Alaska as part of the United States. Indeed, they have been a part of Portugal far longer than either of those two areas, acquired in the nineteenth century, have been parts of the United States.

It seems to me that progress depends upon leaving Portugal alone to deal with its problems in Africa in its own way. I think Portugal is dealing with them intelligently. I believe that to interfere with Portugal's handling of the matter will result in producing chaos in Portuguese Africa and revolution in the Iberian Peninsula. Neither of these consequences seems to me to be to the interest of the United States.

I turn now to South Africa. Here is a country with which it seems to me pure idiocy to sever economic, cultural, or other relations because we do not like its internal arrangements of franchise. We cannot change those arrangements. The entire effort of the British Empire at the height of its power was unable to change them. The British threw in the towel, and the towel is still thrown in, so far as the British are concerned.

The Afrikaners are about as tough a people as exist anywhere in the world. They are not going to be intimidated by economic sanctions, by alleged moral disapproval, or by the cutting off of any kind of communication.

What will happen is the inevitable softening of policy within South Africa through time.

I believe very strongly in the wisdom of leaving the problems of the future to the future. It was the great folly of Chief Justice Roger Taney's tenure as Chief Justice of the United States that he undertook to solve the slavery question for the whole future in the United States. He made a royal mess of the effort. Thereby he helped to produce the Civil War. I believe he set back the whole course of race relationships by a century.

Let our grandchildren deal with the problems in their wisdom and in their time. Although at present some of them are silly, on the whole they are brighter than we are, and I think they will do a better job with their problems than we shall do if we try to deal with them ourselves by preempting solutions.

It seems futile to snipe at a great country such as South Africa. Where do we get by refusing them arms that are highly necessary for their self-defense? They do not need these arms to intimidate their own black inhabitants. They do not need them at all. They can make all they need of armaments of that type. Their needs pertain to the larger and more complex types of armaments required for protection against serious aggression which might come from outside of Africa. I think it is silly to persevere in our policy of restricting such arms for South Africa.

Now we come to Rhodesia, which is the principal focus of our inquiry. I have been interested in the Rhodesian question, very much interested in it, for the last four years. First, I will deal with the question of whether Rhodesia is independent or not, which seems

The Vast External Realm

to me a lawyer's question. There I was about to say something uncomplimentary about lawyers, but then I remembered that I am one, and I am not going to denigrate my own profession.

The question whether Britain should, and on what terms might, grant independence to Rhodesia misses the essential operational reality. Britain had no power, and has no power, to grant or withhold Rhodesian independence. Rhodesia's independence of Britain is an established fact.

The dispute between Rhodesia and Britain focused on procedure for amending certain items in the Rhodesian constitution.

The British official mind became befuddled by the concept of Parliament's supremacy. That idea has operational reality for the United Kingdom itself, where the instruments of administration are subject to Parliament's controls. In view of Parliament's lack of leverage concerning the civil service, the courts, the police, the armed forces, the budget, revenue, commerce, or whatnot in Rhodesia, the idea of parliamentary supremacy projected to that land was an empty abstraction.

Rhodesia moved in 1965 to bring technicalities into line with operational realities by assuming full custody of its own constitution. It employed a power manifestly at its disposal, irrespective of the London government's acquiescence or objection. The action did not create the fact. It only registered the fact.

The British Government invoked a parliamentary enactment which purportedly convened to it plenary powers to deal with the situation: It issued an order-in-council. That document purportedly abolished the governing structure in Rhodesia, assigned absolute control to the government in London, reduced Rhodesia to the status of a crown colony which it had never been—and made the British-appointed figure-head governor in Salisbury a surrogate overlord of the land.

The provisions were fictitious. A more bizarre instance of fantasy decked out in trappings of law can scarcely be imagined.

To determine the pattern of rulership in another country requires conquering it. The British had neither appetite nor capabilities for doing anything of the sort. Nothing was farther from Prime Minister Harold Wilson's resourceful imagination than the intention to invade, to subjugate, to pacify, and to run Rhodesia.

International sanctions were what the British counted on to bail their policy out of bankruptcy. Wholesale commercial restrictions were to be a substitute for the war which the British lacked heart and means to fight.

We live in curious times. The British found the United Nations Security Council in a mood to be gulled. Chorusing anticolonial clichés, assorted governments vowed to help Britain reduce a self-governing territory to crown colony status. British misrepresentation of the background and British misinformation about the prospects were accepted without question. When it came to a matter of declaring Rhodesia to constitute a threat to the peace, so as to rationalize application of mandatory sanctions under article 41 of the charter, the step was taken without the adducing of a scintilla of corroborating evidence.

The actions which have been taken are, of course, in derogation of the charter itself. The powers authorized by chapter VII have been invoked not for the proper purpose of preserving peace but for doing something expressly forbidden by paragraph 7 of article 2 of the charter, which states that the United Nations is to keep hands off matters essentially within the domestic jurisdiction of states.

The idea of using commercial restrictions as a substitute for war in getting control over somebody else's country is a persistent and mischievous superstition in the conduct of international affairs. As in other instances, it has proved delusory in the Rhodesian case.

The results, all contraproductive, have been to encourage the British in impeding a settlement with Rhodesia by insisting on untenable conditions, to solidify the Rhodesian electorate's support of the regime, to push Rhodesia sharply rightward in political outlook, to slow up economic progress for the Rhodesian blacks, and to make the United States improvidently dependent on the Soviet Union for chromite.

In view of the manifest failure of economic sanctions, the question for this government now concerns next steps.

One theoretic possibility is a resort to direct hostilities under article 42 of the charter, as urged by some black African governments.

That, of course, seems to me to be absolutely out of the question. Britain has no will or means for such a venture. I cannot imagine this government's letting itself get involved in hostilities certain to encompass all of southern Africa—a multifarious, remote, difficult area equal to a dozen Californias in size. To blunder into war in southern Africa would have a divisive effect on our society measurelessly greater than Vietnam has had.

An alternate idea is to extend sanctions to all southern Africa. That is a scheme for redeeming folly by compounding it. Even if our government were to take leave of its senses and go along in such an undertaking, the British, I am sure, could be counted on to veto it. They are not about to cut off their lucrative trade with South Africa. In this respect at least, they have not lost perspective about means and ends.

What else? A few souls, reflecting little familiarity and no competence regarding what they are talking about, have urged invocation of section 5(b) of the Trading-with-the-Enemy Act, as amended, or some other and hypothetical act of Congress, with undefined provisions, as a measure for what they paradoxically call disengagement from southern Africa.

The only sure calculable result would be to provide a golden opportunity for capital from other countries, including especially South Africa, to take over extensive American corporate properties, operations, and markets at distress prices.

I do not see any way, just as I do not see any reason, for pressing further into the bog to which British folly, abetted by our own improvidence, has brought us.

I have heard three sorts of arguments on behalf of continuing sanctions. None of them strikes me as having even a shadow of validity.

The first such argument rests on a concept germane to public relations rather than to foreign policy soundly considered. The gist is that persistence will garner moral credits for us among black African governments.

I reject any argument for persisting in folly in hope of applause. In this instance I think the argument is downright patronizing. It rests on a premise that other governments can be fobbed off with tokenism.

Some of the black African governments have discerned the sterility of sanctions all along and insisted that war would be necessary if the purpose of redesigning the government in Rhodesia were to be realized.

If we are not willing to go down that avenue—and I am devoutly hopeful and substantially sure that we are not—then the dignified course is to tell the black African governments concerned that they saw the matter correctly at the outset; that for manifest good reasons we are not of a will to take the steps necessary for that purpose; that the folly of economic hostilities under a guise of preserving peace has proved folly enough; that we are not in a mood to go as far as the ultimate foolishness of making war in the name of evading it; that, in reason, we must abandon a purpose that is beyond our jurisdiction anyway.

The second sort of argument for persisting in sanctions is a hope that somehow, in some unascertainable future through developments not now foreseeable, sanctions may produce deterioration of conditions to a point where Rhodesia's blacks will be incited to rise up against the regime and thus ignite war in southern Africa.

In hope of inducing the tradedy of war, this argument would have us cling to a policy originated ostensibly for the purpose of avoiding war. A more corrupted logic is hard to imagine.

The third argument for going on and on with sanctions is one uttered by a British Government spokesman at a meeting of the United Nations General Assembly's Trusteeship Committee about two weeks ago.

While sanctions have proved inefficacious for the purpose of forcing the Rhodesian Government to submit to being redesigned by others, they have had, according to this version, very important side effects in other directions in that they have denied Rhodesia the degree of economic development and outside capital investment necessary to the territory's economy if it is not to stagnate. So long as sanctions are maintained, Rhodesia's economy will never attain buoyancy. Thus he argued.

The prediction is at variance with observable trends. As its worst aspect, however, the argument is based not on principle but on malice.

Sanctions, ostensibly designed for preserving peace,

become a method of waging a mean war on prosperity. Impoverishment becomes a goal for international collaboration. The ethic of vengeance takes charge.

One feels a touch of pity for the abjectness to which an old ally's policy has come. If we cannot dissuade the British from so shabby a goal, at least we should not feel impelled to accompany them further.

The question is how to get out of sanctions. We can and should do so by unilateral action, if necessary, as well it may be.

One trouble is that the charter does not take into account the eventuality of sanctions coming a cropper. Neither does the United Nations Participation Act. Back at the time of their origin, almost a quarter century ago, it simply was not foreseen that chapter VII would ever be invoked with such disregard for principles and practicalty as we see in the Rhodesian instance.

It would be unwise and unnecessary to hold that the United States can extricate itself from sanctions only by the procedure by which it entered—to wit, by a vote of the Security Council susceptible of veto by any one of the permanent members.

I can scarcely imagine that the Soviet Union would fail to veto an action designed to free us from the predicament which we are in with respect to the availability and pricing of chromite ore.

My own belief is that the residual power remains with the United States, and rests specifically with the President, to determine whether and when an action under chapter VII has failed and thereupon to declare an end to our obligation to continue the action.

I understand that the continued presence of the U.S. consular establishment at Salisbury is a matter of concern to the subcommittee in view of the prospective proclamation of a Rhodesian republic.

The allegation is that failure to close the consulate might be construed as a weakening of resolve to maintain sanctions and even as a prefigurement of eventual diplomatic recognition.

I do not see either of these results as a necessary corollary of keeping open the consulate.

If the conclusion were otherwise, however, I would ask: So what?

It is high time to get the folly of sanctions over and done with.

As for the question of eventual recognition, I am content to leave the matter where the Constitution puts it—in the President's discretion, subject to coordination with the Senate serving as a sort of council of state.

On September 25, 1969, the Senate acted on Senate Resolution 205, introduced by Senators Cranston and Aiken. Its gist is:

> That it is the sense of the Senate that when the United States recognizes a foreign government and exchanges diplomatic representatives with it, this does not imply that the United States necessarily approves of the form, ideology, or policy of that government.

The yeas were seventy-seven. The nays were three. I call that an impressive majority.

At the Senate Foreign Relations Committee's hearing on June 17, 1969, on Senate Resolution 205, Mr. George H. Aldrich, Acting Legal Adviser of the Department of State, appearing in support of the resolution, said: "The proposed resolution reflects the established position of the United States that recognition of a foreign government does not imply approval of that government's domestic policies or the means by which it came to power."

Good. The executive also goes along in what I regard as a sound approach. The proper source of advice is the Senate, and it has spoken. The executive branch seems to concur. Without venturing a specific prediction, I think I see signs of the end of an error.

Now, Mr. Chairman, may I conclude by reading two paragraphs here.

One is from the *London Financial Times* of November 11. It reads as follows:

> Anyone visiting Rhodesia today might be pardoned for forgetting that the country has now been fighting an economic war for four years. Visible signs of the battle scars of the sanctions campaign are indeed hard to find. Instead, one finds an economy enjoying its most rapid growth rate for some fifteen years, with all sectors, without exception, reaching forward to new record indications. Current indications suggest a real terms growth in 1969 of the order of 10 percent. That is allowing for 2½ to 3 percent rate of the price inflation.

I finally conclude by going back almost a hundred years to read a statement by a great British Prime Minister, Lord Salisbury, who said:

Southern Africa

The commonest error in politics is sticking to the carcasses of dead policies. When a mast falls overboard, you do not try to save a rope here and a spar there, in memory of their former utility; you cut away the hamper altogether. And it should be the same with a policy. But it is not so. We cling to the shred of an old policy after it has been torn to pieces, and to the shadow of the shred after the rag itself has been torn away. And therefore it is that we are now in perplexity.

Canada: "Stern Daughter of the Voice of God"

Americans take Canada for granted, and Canadians are forever saying so. By this they mean that Americans assume Canada to be bestowed as a right and accept this bounty, as they do air, without thought or appreciation. Perhaps they do; and perhaps they should. For, if it were not taken as a bounty of nature, America might not grasp Canada at all for sheer difficulty in figuring out what Canada is.

By Canada, one means Canadians. The land is clear enough on the map; the economy, in innumerable

Neighbors Taken for Granted, Canada and the United States, edited by Livingston T. Merchant, published for the School of Advanced International Studies of the Johns Hopkins University (New York: Frederick A. Praeger, 1966), Chapter VI. (Title of the chapter taken from Wordsworth, "Ode to Duty.")

prospectuses; and both are much appreciated by visitors and investors. What Americans take as the bounty of nature is the people—not the politicians, not the press, not something called Canadian culture or cultures—but Canadians.

Americans and, perhaps, Canadians, too, do not have much of an idea what this generic noun Canadian describes, if it describes anything. One who has relatives in Canada is the most bemused of all, for he confidently believes that his relatives are "typical" Canadians. Yet the one sure thing about this belief is that it must be wrong. If his relatives are British Canadians they throw no light on French Canadians, and vice versa. If they live in the Maritimes, they are quite different from the inhabitants of the Prairie Provinces or British Columbia. And if they are what is left of the United Empire Loyalists of Upper Canada, they are unique. When Prime Minister Lester Pearson tells us that despite regionalism the people of Canada are "essentially Canadian," he unhappily does not enlighten us further.

Americans, then, are uninformed about Canadians, but infinitely well disposed, and, too often, infuriatingly patronizing. A poll taken in the United States would bring out the unanimous opinion that Canadians are fine, straightforward, hard-working, intelligent, courageous, great hockey players, and—God forgive us!—the highest encomium, "just like Americans." They are ideal neighbors. We would rather they lived in Canada than live there ourselves, or have our dear friends, the Vietnamese, do so. For the knight of romance, a wise man has written, it was not enough to say that his lady was a very fine girl. You must agree that she was the finest that God ever had made or would make, or you must fight. So it is with Mr. Pearson. He writes in *Foreign Affairs*:

> A few Americans know Canada well, but many do not know it even a little. This irks us. Indeed a major irritant in our relations with the United States is the tendency of some Americans simply to take Canadians for granted.[1]

The remedy for this deplorable situation is, of course, greater knowledge. But is greater knowledge wise? Another, and, perhaps, more percipient Canadian, Robert Fulford, considering the same problem in the *Toronto Star*, concludes:

> Americans, we have argued for years, don't show enough interest in Canada.
>
> But now this is changing. American magazines are developing a persistent as opposed to a fitful appetite for material about Canada. Perhaps this means that in the future the Americans will begin to understand us.
>
> When that happens, we may well find ourselves looking back on the days of their ignorance with acute nostalgia. For surely those Americans who study Canada will sooner or later discover both our assumed moral superiority and the pitiful reality that lies behind it. When they do their laughter may be hard to bear.[2]

1. Lester B. Pearson, "Good Neighborhood," *Foreign Affairs,* January, 1965, p. 255.
2. Robert Fulford, "Canada's Moral Pride," *The Toronto Daily Star,* December 3, 1964, p. 43.

"Stern Daughter of the Voice of God"

What does he mean by Canadian "assumed moral superiority," and what is its relevance? It begins with the fact that Canadians of all regions suffer from the common failing of all people everywhere, not excepting the United States—parochialism. Its virulence, until recently, at least, was pre-eminent in Quebec. In the light of this parochialism we must examine something about which one has heard a good deal from Ottawa; that is, from politicians and publicists rather than one's Canadian friends. Canadians, we are told, have in the culture of their "two founding peoples" something which must be safeguarded from engulfing vulgarity from south of the border. The French Canadians, writes Mr. Pearson, possess a "culture which is French both in its source and in its quality. Yet they are completely Canadian. After the original Indians and Eskimos, they were the first Canadians."[3]

What he says about the culture of the "first" Canadians after the "original" Canadians is doubtless justified by what we might call political license. Undoubtedly the French *voyageurs* brought with them to Canada the French ideas and Catholicism of the sixteenth and seventeenth centuries. Their descendants still speak a form of French related to that currently used in literate France as the language of the less-penetrated portions of the southern Appalachian Mountains is related to that spoken today in literate England. But if there have been French Canadian contributions to French culture they have had scant recog-

---

3. "Good Neighborhood," p. 253.

nition in French scientific or literary journals, in French music, or in French galleries.

The story is different on the English-speaking side. Though not comparable to the contributions of the Netherlands, Belguim, or Denmark, Canadian nuclear scientists have done notable work at Chalk River. Canadian writers have far surpassed Ralph Connor's once popular book *The Sky Pilot*. Canadian orchestras and ballet are good; and Riopelle is an important painter, even though, like Whistler and Picasso, he has found an atmosphere congenial to his art outside his own country. The Canadian "Seven" of an earlier day were also painters worthy of respect. Yet, when all is said, one cannot quarrel with Mr. Fulford's summing up: "In the arts and sciences we are so far behind them [the Americans] that no meaningful comparison can be made."

From this conclusion, he passes to another: ". . . but we at least see ourselves as morally superior to the Americans. We cling to this as the white trash cling to segregation. Heaven help us if it ever vanishes and we must see ourselves naked."

The origin of this bit of folklore lies, Mr. Fulford finds not surprisingly, in the minds of the believers: "The trouble is that the idea of Canadian moral superiority is hard to sustain if you take into account the facts of Canadian history and Canadian society. Most of us solve this problem in the most obvious way. We ignore the facts."

They are aided by scrupulously following a "policy of selective recall" and "know, for instance, that in the 1930s England practiced something called 'ap-

peasement' and the Americans . . . 'isolationism.' "
These two powers were responsible for World War
II, even though "Canada's government was more ap-
peasement-prone than England's in the 1930's, and
Canadian statesmen as a whole made mid-western
Americans look, by comparison, like international-
ists." Indeed, the folklore about war goes further.
"When the Americans have shown reluctance to
enter a war in which we have been involved, we have
regarded them as shirkers. When they have armed
themselves carefully against their enemies and ours,
we have helpfully pointed out that they are warmon-
gers."

Selective recall operates equally well in the political
field to sustain Canada's "moral pride":

Canadians have never mounted a foreign aid program
that is better than niggardly, yet we have always felt it
our duty to criticize the more generous Americans. . . .
We have systems of public housing and social security
which are sensationally inferior to those of the Americans, yet we believe that we are more open to liberal
ways than they are. . . .

Our federal Parliament has for several years found it
all but impossible to pass the simplest measures. In the
last eighteen months the United States Congress has
passed bold new legislation. Yet every schoolboy knows
(because his history teacher tells him) that the British
parliamentary system as practised in Canada is vastly superior to the unwieldy and backward system of the
Americans.

We English-speaking and French-speaking Canadians
have rarely if ever shown any genuine interest in under-

199

standing each other, yet we have for generations told the Americans exactly how to settle their monumentally challenging race issue.

Canadians feel about their moral superiority as the authors of the American Declaration of Independence did almost two hundred years ago: "We hold these truths to be self-evident!"

And yet, one doubts. Has not Mr. Fulford been too harsh? Surely these views are familiar. One hears and reads them often. But from the mouth or pen of a professional or political Canadian. Not from one's friends.

Fortunately, there is something approaching evidence—proof would be too strong a word—that this is true. Last year, in *Maclean's* magazine, a leading Canadian publication, Blair Fraser analyzed a remarkable survey by the Canadian Peace Research Institute, a private Canadian corporation supported by 25,000 contributors.[4] Mr. Fraser, who enjoys a wide reputation in Canada as an experienced, perceptive, and fair-minded political commentator, discussed the Institute's conclusion that on matters of foreign policy "a majority of Canadians differ sharply from the majority of politicians, regardless of party."

Before examining the nature of the differences, one should state at once that the mere fact of the difference should not be surprising. If no difference existed, it would mean, to a near certainty, that the politicians were following, not leading, popular opinion. To be

4. "Our Quiet War Over Peace: Politicians vs. The People," *Maclean's,* January 23, 1965, p. 18.

leaders they must be ahead of, not behind, the led; in the minority of leaders not in the majority of followers. But to be leaders they must by definition have followers going in the same direction, though more slowly.

Popular opinion does not deal in niceties. Its loyalties are roughhewn. One gets an informing line on the ethos of a people—or, to be more earthy, upon its savvy about the world around us—by knowing whether it grasps the fact of a deeply divided world, and suspects what it is divided about, or believes that the new nations will lead their sinful, developed brothers to peace, prosperity, and reconciliation through the United Nations. The Research Institute has sought to penetrate these mysteries in a sophisticated and percipient way. Its conclusions are that the Canadian public and its politicians are far apart, and suggest that the latter have only recently become aware of it.

Let us start with five related questions, the answers to which were reported both by totals and by national origin and other groupings. First, the bare outlines:

Policy	National Opinion for	Politicians' Opinion for
	(in per cent)	
Hard line against Communist bloc	41	4
Peaceful coexistence	33	73
Nuclear arms for Canada	45	27
More foreign aid now	12	73
Strengthening the United Nations	46	55

The Vast External Realm

Equally singificant is the fact that the answers of neither the "informed" group nor the two national origin groups differ substantially on most questions from opinion as a whole. Perhaps the most startling revelation of this survey is the radical difference it portrays from earlier single, general question polls. In 1961, 86 per cent of Canadians thought that the United Nations did a "good" or "fair" job. Now only 46 per cent are in favor of "strengthening" it. Conclusions from these data are tricky to make and can be deceptive. But they do not bear out the view which Mr. Fraser believes some Canadians have had of themselves as "leading the march toward peace, stalwart and loyal supporters of the United Nations, conscientious objectors to nuclear weapons, generous donors of aid to less-favored nations, standard bearers in any movement toward disarmament and peaceful coexistence."[5]

But, one must insist again, it would be grossly unfair to pin this view of themselves on private Canadians generally. The survey places it where it belongs—on the politicians. For them there is a strong incentive to seek success and reputation in external rather than internal affairs. The extreme delicacy of the relations between Canada's "two founding peoples" has quite understandably made the present policy of "cooperative federalism" concentrate on keeping the country united and cautious in domestic innovation. When a nettle has been grasped, as in the

5. The material in this paragraph and the preceding one has been drawn from Mr. Fraser's article cited above.

recent decision on a national flag, one gladly gives full marks to the courage of the prime minister and the good sense of his fellow countrymen. We must humbly put it down to our good luck and not our merit that Betsy Ross was not a congressional committee.

In "the vast external realm," however, the Canadian politician can and does appear with more panache. At first, his role was seen as a loving reconciler of common mother and long lost son. But as the consequences of World War II extended the Statute of Westminster and the British Empire faded into the Commonwealth, the role changed radically. It became more ambitious; its purposes and medium more adapted to Canada's potentialities and position in the postwar world. A leading Canadian politician has remarked that a representative of a middle-sized power has advantages: he is listened to, but not held responsible for results; thus, he can acquire reputation and honors, while blame for failure goes to those possessed of power and means. What role, then, beckons him? It has not been a smooth or altogether satisfactory one.

Canada, writes Mr. Pearson, "in the troubled years since the last great war . . . has developed a special interest in international peace-keeping in many of the world's trouble spots and has played a leading part— with men, equipment, money and ideas—in the effort to make peace-keeping activities effective." [6] At the

6. "Good Neighborhood," p. 259.

same time, "Canada played a leading part in the formation of the NATO alliance and from the outset has been a strong advocate of the development of an Atlantic community embracing North America and the European nations from which came the forebears of most Canadians and Americans. We believed in this concept, but we would lose interest if it degenerated into merely an old-fashioned military alliance directed by three or four of its most powerful members."[7] To hold Canadian interest, NATO must be "genuinely collective."[8] General de Gaulle, the head of one of Canada's "forebears," would not express his interest in NATO in just the same way, nor has he, like Mr. Pearson, "developed a special interest in international peace-keeping." This illustrates one of the many difficulties of combining Canada's "leading role" and her "special interest."

There are others, too. Some of them, perhaps, lie behind the warning that Canadians would lose interest in NATO should it become "an old-fashioned military alliance." The plain fact, of course, is that NATO is a military alliance. Its purpose was and is to deter and, if necessary, to meet the use of Russian military power or the fear of its use in Europe. This purpose is pretty old-fashioned. Perhaps to avoid this stigma, Canadian draftsmen had Article 2 inserted in the Treaty. That article calls for joint action by the signatories in economic and cultural fields as well as in the military; but despite studies by two groups of

7. *Ibid.,* p. 258.
8. *Ibid.,* p. 259.

"Stern Daughter of the Voice of God"

"wisemen" guided by Canadians, no promising areas were discovered. Effective economic and cultural co-operation requires a more broadly based group. So Mr. Pearson concludes on a note of doubt: Canadians as members of NATO will "continue to bear our share of the burden of collective defense, so long as it is genuinely collective." [9]

A month later, when Mr. Pearson returned to the subject of NATO in February, 1965, his doubts about NATO had grown. He still believed "in the Atlantic coalition," "but less as a defense coalition and more as a foundation for a closely cooperating political and economic community. Unfortunately there is little political and economic cement these days for Atlantic unity. . . . The best result would be to come closer together, organically, on the old Treaty basis. But that is impossible at the moment if we wish to include the France of General de Gaulle. And certainly in Canada it is impossible to contemplate an Atlantic coalition without France." [10] (Mr. Pearson is not the first political leader to discover how much foreign policy can become a function of domestic politics.)

The February conclusion is even more doubtful and frustrated than that of January: "This means that a country like Canada will have to consider very seriously whether the contribution we are presently making overseas to NATO is the best use of our

9. *Ibid.*
10. Excerpts from an address to the Canadian Club of Ottawa by The Honorable Lester B. Pearson. Press Release, February 10, 1965, p. 4.

resources for the defense of peace."[11] Clearly, the outlook for Canada's "leading part" in NATO appears
dim.

Unhappily, the prospect for her "special interest
in international peace-keeping" does not seem much
brighter to Mr. Pearson:

> Next there is the United Nations, full support of which,
> as I have been saying for twenty years, is a basic founda-
> tion of our foreign policy.
> I still believe this, but I think the time has come—
> especially in the light of the current crisis in the Assem-
> bly—to have a long, hard look at the organization.[12]

One may suggest that the "long, hard look" should
be directed not only at the organization but at the
problems which international peace-keeping will increasingly pose for Canada in her own integrity, her
political alignment, and her ultimate purposes.

First, the country must be clear on the relative importance of the sort of international peace-keeping
which has been the "special interest" of Canadian
politicians. These measures are peripheral and ancil-
lary to the policies, organization, and power which
have been created by and under the leadership of the
United States to maintain security for free societies in
a divided world. No responsible Canadian politician
would for a moment question this directly. But the
essential, fundamental power and purpose is not

11. *Ibid.,* p. 5.
12. *Ibid.*

strengthened by deprecating NATO as a "defense coalition," by questioning Canada's continued contribution to it, by relying upon Europe as "strong," and by believing that "the Communists are less obstreperous." [13]

Furthermore, "action to contain local or regional disputes" (Mr. Pearson's phrase for U.N. peace-keeping) can only succeed if the forces instigating the dispute are weak enough to be contained by such forces as the U.N. can raise and finance over Communist opposition and (often) neutral debilitating conditions. In Korea and Vietnam, the power and finance had and have to be supplied by the victim and the United States.

Success, it is true, came at the time of Suez, and was crowned with the laurel of a Nobel Peace Prize. The falling out of allies in the most inept diplomatic episode since Munich furnished the opportunity. But when, through a series of moves bizarre on all sides, the United States found itself separated from Britain and France and joined with the Soviet Union in demanding that military action cease, the major act of "peace-keeping" had been done. The U.N.'s function was to tidy up the mess—a useful job, but one which left a disagreeable impression that the troublemakers had ended up on top and been sprinkled with holy water.

Finally, a Canadian politician anxious to lead in international peace-keeping must in fairness to his

13. *Ibid.*, pp. 4, 5.

fellow citizens face up to the questions: Who will control these operations and what will their purposes be? Mr. Pearson has been frank about this: "Of course, any policy decisions with respect to the U.N.'s peace-keeping capacity can be taken only in and by the United Nations itself. I hope that progress may be made here, but it will be difficult in an atmosphere of cold-war and neo-colonial suspicion." [14]

If one asks who will control the United Nations, Mr. Pearson answers that, too: "The domination through numbers is becoming more and more African and Asian." [15] He finds Canada's position appealing to this new majority: "Our position [is] one of respectable importance, while we are not big enough to alarm anybody or dominate anybody's way of life. We have American plumbing without American power. This makes us attractive to many; especially new and underdeveloped states." [16] Doubtless Canada's attraction would be even greater, should her government in reconsidering "the best use of [their] resources in the defense of peace" decide to move further from "an atmosphere of cold-war and neo-colonial suspicion" which many new states associate with NATO.

Perhaps Canadian leaders would do well to think even more deeply than they have about where they may be led by the new dominant majority of the U.N.

14. "Good Neighborhood," p. 259.
15. Address to Canadian Club, p. 5.
16. *Ibid.,* p. 2.

to whom Canada is thought to be so attractive. What does "U.N. peace-keeping" involve? The answer comes from Mr. Pearson's pen: "What it involves, in essence, is international action to contain local or regional disputes and to create the conditions in which solutions can be negotiated at the political level."

Local or regional disputes are what the Communist and neutralist members of the United Nations describe by the euphemism "wars of national liberation." The Soviet- and Chinese-mounted attack on Korea was a "war of national liberation," and the attempted *coup d'état* in Lebanon in 1958 would doubtless have been called the same thing if U.S. Marines had not landed and scotched it. This is what Sukarno calls his aggression against Malaysia; Nasser and Nkrumah, the Communist-subsidized vendetta in the Congo. Most recently, it is the name given by Chou En-lai and Ho Chi Minh to their decade of subversive and guerrilla war against Vietnam.

Canadian officials in pursuit of their peace-keeping functions on the International Control Commission have recently been made brutally aware of this last. To their great credit, they have said so with complete candor. Thus Paul Martin, Canadian Secretary of State for External Affairs, on February 18, 1965:

In its special report of June, 1962, the International Commission in Vietnam, after careful analysis of a large number of South Vietnamese complaints, came to the conclusion that armed and unarmed personnel, arms, munitions, and other supplies, had been sent from North Vietnam into South Vietnam with the object of supporting, organizing, and carrying out hostile activities, including armed attack directed against the armed forces and administration of South Vietnam. This same report also concluded that the North Vietnamese authorities had allowed their territories to be used for inciting, encouraging, and supporting hostile activities in South Vietnam aimed at the overthrow of the South Vietnamese administration.

It is against the background of these established facts that recent events must be judged. . . .

The United States Government has made it clear that it seeks no wider war. In responding to provocation, its military action was limited and specific, in being confined to military targets forming an integral part of the network by which the North steers and supplies the rebel military forces in the South. As proof of its intentions, the United States has taken prompt action in informing the Security Council of what had happened.

In some quarters, a new Geneva conference has been urged. . . . The machinery for such a conference exists within the framework of the 1954 agreements. As far as Canada is concerned, I have stated on many occasions that we are prepared to participate in such a conference provided it is held in the right conditions. But so long as the North Vietnamese authorities persist in their policy of intervention in the South, it is difficult to see what useful contribution could be made to the peace and stability of Vietnam by a new conference.[17]

17. Excerpts from an address to the Board of Evangelism and Social Service of the United Church of Canada, February 18, 1965. Release No. 65/4 of Department of External Affairs.

"Stern Daughter of the Voice of God"

This is an admirable recognition of reality in a current, critical situation; it could well lead to further profound consideration of the prospect of Afro-Asian–controlled international peace-keeping policy.

For a long time, Soviet leaders have been most explicit that military aggression, when called a war of national liberation, is wholly compatible with their conception of peaceful coexistence. Hence, instigation and supplying of attempts to overthrow non-Communist governments by force is always proper, while help to the victim is a violation of the U.N. Charter, an interference in the internal affairs of another country, and warmongering. Hence, also, the Soviet-Sukarno-Nasser interpretation of a solution to such a dispute "negotiated at the political level" is pretty obvious. One does not require an overly suspicious nature to foresee such action in the present composition of the United Nations developing into a "die easy" policy, in which non-Communist regimes will be succeeded by Communist or Communist-front controls. Can anyone doubt that U.N. containment of the "local or regional disputes" in Malaysia and Vietnam would have instantaneous and adverse effect on the governments of both countries? Can one have much doubt of conflict between such a policy and the more basic and rugged peace-keeping and freedom-keeping responsibilities which fall so heavily on the United States? Finally, can one doubt that ambition to lead in U.N. peace-keeping, as the U.N. is presently constituted, and still maintain a "leading role" in "a genuinely collective" NATO could create ambivalence and ambiguity in attitude and performance?

So one ends with mingled doubt and hope that political leaders in Canada and the United States will be able to work as closely and effectively together in their relations with the world outside their continent as the people of both countries wish them to. One hopes that they can "show understanding and respect for each other's views," [18] and still retain fidelity to their own. But this is not a mere matter of good-will; nor is it foreordained. If it is to be achieved, Americans must not take Canadians for granted. But something more is needed. Canadians must not take Americans for granted, either.

18. "Good Neighborhood," p. 261.

Part Six ⋘

In Memoriam

The Supreme Artist

My former chief, President Truman, has called Sir Winston Churchill the greatest public figure of our age. This is an understatement. One would, I think, have to go back, certainly in the English-speaking world, four centuries to find his equal.

For his equal could not merely be a soldier, statesman, or orator, or all three. Equality would require the ability to create that "romantic attachment" which, as Sir John Neale has pointed out, existed between the English people and the great Queen. Sir John has also drawn the comparison: "It was an attachment for which I think the closest parallel in our history is that between Englishmen and Winston Churchill in our own time."

Certainly, in my own country no leader has inspired

From *Churchill by His Contemporaries—An Observer Appreciation,* edited by *The Observer* (London: Hodder and Stoughton, 1965).

in his own lifetime this "romantic attachment." General Washington, great as he was, inspired respect and, all too briefly, gratitude. Bonaparte inspired romantic devotion to be sure; but his influence was divisive and disastrous and he had about him an aura of falsity and self-seeking.

"What is the explanation?" asks Sir John, and answers. "As in the case of Winston Churchill, undoubtedly the supreme art and deliberate policy of the Queen." Both Elizabeth and Churchill needed, and used, all their superb qualities of heart and brain, their indomitable courage, inexhaustible energy, their magnanimity and good sense, to bring their country through its two periods of darkest peril.

But these might not have been enough without their "supreme art." It was this which fused and multiplied all the rest to inspire the English people with the reckless, gay, and confident courage to enable them twice, under adored leaders, to face and fight alone the greatest military and ideological powers of two ages.

Here, raised to its highest, is the leadership which alone can call forth from a free people what cannot be commanded. Neither courage, nor right decisions, nor speaking good words is enough. Art, great art, transforms all these into something different and superlative. What Churchill did was great: how he did it was equally so. Neither action nor style could have accomplished the result alone. Both were needed.

Not only was the content of his speeches wise and right but they were prepared with that infinite capacity for taking pains which is said to be genius. So was his appearance; his attitudes and gestures, his use of all the artifices to get his way, from wooing and cajolery, through powerful advocacy to bluff bullying —all were carefully adjusted to the need. To call this acting is quite inadequate. Acting is a mode infinitely variable and adjustable. What we are speaking of is a transformation, a growth, and a permanent change of personality. Napoleon understood this. So did Roosevelt. Washington did not.

Churchill mastered it. Its manifestation was dramatic and romantic—the endless energy which took him into everything and every place, the siren suit, the indomitable V sign for victory, the cigar for imperturbability, and so on. Here, too, he and Elizabeth moved together. In his speeches the bedrock of sense and necessity was clothed, as in hers, with romanticism. Of all the words which must, forever, move English and French hearts are those closing his broadcast, in October, 1940, to the French people:

> Good night then: sleep to gather strength for the morning. For the morning will come. Brightly will it shine on the brave and true, kindly upon all who suffer for the cause, glorious upon the tombs of heroes. Thus will shine the dawn. *Vive la France!*

And Elizabeth, at a no less critical moment, with the Armada at sea, clothed resolution in romance:

> I know I have the body of a weak and feeble woman, but I have the heart and stomach of a King, and of a King of England, too.

In Memoriam

Here is romantic emotion, not for its own sake, but as a vital element of action directed towards result.

Sir Winston's power and art were not reserved for great public occasions alone. Anyone who has sat with him in private negotiation has marvelled at his strength and his art. He was at once composer, conductor, and soloist. But the virtuoso never lost touch with the basic theme. He would, in a flash, close at the point closest to the flood tide of his strength. In the meantime every art had been exercised to soften the heart, move the emotions, and intimidate. All those who had a part in the negotitations over the Atlantic Sea Command of NATO can contribute supporting evidence.

Sir Winston Churchill respected vigorous opposition. He enjoyed stratagems, and thought well of one who saw through and countered them, without causing him too much inconvenience. It was not hard to please him here because his stratagems were not obscure and his purposes were right. Though others know far better, I suspect that he enjoyed gaiety and controversy, in equal proportions.

I remember an example of this at a dinner he gave in Washington in January, 1953, for President Truman and a few others. An unguarded remark of Sir Winston's led to his trial before the President, acting as Commissioner of the Pearly Gates Authority, for admission. This, Sir Winston insisted, must be in accordance with the common law of England. So the company began selecting from the pages of history a jury of his peers. By the time the examination on *voir dire* and selection had got as far as Alexander the Great, Thucydides, Herodotus, Aristotle, Caesar, and Marcus Aurelius, the Prime Minister waived a jury. But he insisted that he would never waive habeas corpus. The Commissioner recommended admission without further proceedings.

This capacity for vigorous enjoyment, and another far rarer one, he shared with Elizabeth, each in accordance with the conceptions of their different times—the capacity to hold their own imperious natures under disciplined control. Lord Alanbrooke is authority for the statement that much as Sir Winston pushed, harassed, bullied, and threatened the British chiefs of staff, he never overruled them. He knew the limits of his proper and constitutional role, and of theirs. Lord Alanbrooke also ventured the opinion that if Hitler had acted in the same way the outcome of the war might have been different.

Underlying all of Churchill's nature was his amazing vitality, the life force, that rarest of all gifts, which Lord Keynes told me means in England a strain of Villiers blood. Wherever it comes from, it is rare, and indispensable to leadership in public life. In my own country, the early Adamses had it, and Mr. Truman has it.

It gives staying and working power, good nerves, ability to sleep at any time, and to wake fresh. It is incompatible with the weakest of human emotions, worry and regret, and leaves a fair field for deliberate judg-

In Memoriam

ment. It is the essence of command: and it was, certainly, a Tudor quality. Let Sir Winston be his own
witness:

> Thus, then, on the night of the tenth of May [1940], at
> the outset of this mighty battle, I acquired the chief
> powers in the State . . . Therefore, although impatient
> for the morning, I slept soundly and had no need for
> cheering dreams. Facts are better than dreams.

Ernest Bevin

Ernest Bevin's characteristics as a Foreign Secretary were, as one might expect, closely related to his characteristics as a man.

When one thinks of him, without attempt at ordered analysis, memory first evokes emotion—affection, coupled with trust.

One thinks of a warm and loving nature; a man of modesty, gruff and plain spoken and with equally plain, unsubtle humor;

An honorable man, courageous and loyal to the tips of his stubby fingers.

He had a strong mind, learned quickly, and held vigorously to positions taken.

Deeply ingrained in him was an acute consciousness of the unbroken flow of British life and history and of

For B.B.C. recording on "Mr. Ernest Bevin's Characteristics as a Foreign Secretary" (February 26, 1957).

221

In Memoriam

being an inseparable part of it.

To him this was no metaphor but a living reality.

His predecessors were honored and respected presences, as real to him as the dock workers to whom he had given so much of his life.

He said to me one day, "Last night I was reading a paper of old Salisbury's. He had a lot of sense."

It was plain that he felt Queen Victoria's great Prime Minister and Foreign Secretary at his shoulder, sustaining a successor in the same task of safeguarding Britain.

With such a man relations were intensely personal.

He evoked affection and trust and returned them.

He relied heavily on his professional staff who, as Lord Strang has said, were devoted to him, and often baffled by him.

But policy recommendations, by the time he acted on them, had been deeply tinged by his own thought.

In substance, his policy was to unite and strengthen the Western coalition against Soviet pressure, economic, political, and military.

He conceived of this as a common task at the heart of which lay Anglo-American-French solidarity.

This tripartite relationship was cemented by his courage and integrity and by the trust which he both inspired in his French and American colleagues and gave to them.

222

Hume Wrong

The death of Ambassador Hume Wrong in Ottawa at fifty-nine is a loss which is shared and mourned by Americans with our Canadian neighbors. Those who knew and admired his great qualities of mind and character, his experience in international affairs, his understanding and wise judgment, believed that he had many years of useful service before him. It seemed, too, that his return to Ottawa from Washington to become the second in command in the Department of External Affairs, working with his old friend and colleague, Mr. Lester B. Pearson, had placed him in the ideal position for the use of his great talents. The death of such a man at such a time is in many ways a double loss—a loss to America as well as to Canada, for no one understood better or made a greater contribution to the relations between

The New York Times, January 25, 1954.

223

these two great North American countries—a personal loss to a great company of devoted friends in both countries and a loss to professional colleagues in both countries—and a loss, too, to all in many countries who worked patiently and earnestly at the immensely complicated task of strengthening and uniting the free countries.

Hume Wrong was one of the pioneers of the Canadian Foreign Service, one of that small but extraordinarily brilliant group which included Mr. Lester B. Pearson, Mr. Norman Robertson, Dr. Skelton, and Mr. Justice John Reed. Few countries have been so fortunate in those who formed the traditions of their foreign policy. He entered the service in 1927 when Mr. Vincent Massey brought him to Washington in Canada's first foreign mission outside the Commonwealth. He has served here many times, as well as in London and Geneva, always with a broadening grasp and responsibility. His own background of teaching and scholarship, which was also that of his distinguished father, Mr. George Wrong, disciplined a mind naturally clear and precise. He learned from his grandfather Edward Blake, one of Canada's great statesmen, the possibilities and limitations of leadership in a free and democratic society.

He and I carried on a friendship and a pursuit of common goals which went back on both sides for two generations before us. As I think of our years of work and friendship, the qualities of his which keep coming back to my mind are his goodness and his integrity. There are many able men in this world

Hume Wrong

but not nearly so many—indeed, all too few—of whom
one says, "He is a good man." Hume Wrong was that,
and with it went his invincible integrity. What he
thought was right, that he did—without bitterness,
without aspersions upon a differing view, but without
any compromise of his own conviction.

He will be sadly missed and deeply mourned. He
was a gallant gentleman and an honorable servant of
his country and of mankind.

A Farewell to Daisy Harriman

Each of us who have come here to pay a last tribute of affection and say a long farewell to Daisy Harriman comes drawn by a personal bond formed over the years with our mutual and beloved friend.

My own bond was an inherited one. Well over three-quarters of a century ago as a young woman she and her parents went to St. George's Church in New York, where my father was a very young curate. There they formed a friendship which was passed on to me and continued, warm and loyal, to the end of her long life. So today I pay her a double tribute of admiration and affection.

From her earliest youth Daisy Harriman reached out to life with the joyous embrace of great vitality. This extra gift of the life force itself is, perhaps, the greatest that God gives to his sons and daughters. It

September 5, 1967.

is given not as a reward for virtue, but in a discriminating and mysterious way to a remote ancestor here and there and passed down. Daisy Harriman had it. Sir Winston Churchill had it; old Sam Adams had it. It makes for warriors—and happy warriors—who fight for great causes and to right wrongs.

Daisy Harriman fought to right the wrongs of her time and country: To end child labor, discrimination against women in public life; to end war through the League of Nations; to strengthen the party, as she saw it of the disinherited; to end the disenfranchisement of her fellow citizens in her own hometown. Even when she had entered the period that today only the blunt call old age and was representing her country in Norway, she met the Nazi invader like a veritable lion.

Her great energy, her enormous courage, and her assurance of her own pre-eminence brought her magnanimity. Rarest of the rugged, old-fashioned virtures, one sees it all too seldom now in our capital city; and yet more than anything else it sweetens life around those who possess it. Daisy Harriman fought, and fought hard; but she did not scratch. She presided over tough and searching debate; but not mean innuendo. She never thought the contemptible amusing, but treated it with contempt. Her magnanimity to her opponents—she had no enemies—and friends alike, as well as in the face of all that life dealt her, freshened and sweetened the air about her.

As we say goodby to her, the words *Requiescat in pace* come to our lips and are checked there. Somehow one cannot think of Daisy Harriman resting—and par-

In Memoriam

ticularly in peace—when so much still waits to be done. Perhaps, in the Heavenly City there are no urban problems. Still, from reports, the rule there is said to have an autocratic flavor which might turn her rest to fitful fever. So instead of "Rest in Peace," let us say to her today:

Ride on! Ride on in majesty!
Hark! All the tribes hosanna cry!

William Duncan Herridge

William Duncan Herridge, who died in Ottawa on Sept. 21 after a long illness, was thirty years ago one of the best known and most beloved men in official Washington. The second Canadian Minister to this government (from 1931 to 1935), he succeeded Mr. Vincent Massey in establishing a distinguished line. The ranks of those who cherished him as a friend and admired him as one of the ablest diplomats whom this country has known—although a most unconventional one—are becoming distressingly thin. They will join me in asking your courtesy to pay him our tribute.

The first, central, and all-important fact about Herridge was his vitality. It poured out of him, sometimes as ideas tumbling over one another, sometimes as gaiety, or as physical activity—he was a great fisher-

The Washington Post, October 1, 1961.

man and camper—or as host and conversationalist, or a pretty wild political schemer. Whatever he did was done with verve and often with a good deal of noise. To be with him was to be alive, to be moving, and to be breathless. It was also to be with a man who gave and inspired affection.

Herridge's preparation for a diplomatic role was probably unique in the annals of the art. He was a patent lawyer, and an eminent one, at the Canadian bar. He was also a friend of the Commanding Officer of the Canadian forces in World War I, Lord (Bungo) Byng, who, as Governor General of Canada after the war, Herridge thought had been shabbily treated by the Canadian Liberals in their political maneuverings. This led Herridge to put his very considerable talents at the disposal of Richard C. Bennett (later Lord Bennett), the Conservative leader, in his victorious election campaign of 1930. At the London Imperial Conference Herridge helped devise and draft the system of imperial tariff preferences, as an answer to the American Smoot-Hawley Tariff Act of 1930. Then, marrying the Prime Minister's sister, he came to Washington.

It was a fateful time. The Hoover Administration was about to "straggle to an end in sandy deltas"; and the New Deal, full of promise, and threat for Canada, about to burst upon a shaken world. In the opening years of the New Deal, Herridge played his most brilliant role.

The function of a diplomatic envoy, since the eighteenth century, has been a twofold one—to observe

William Duncan Herridge

and report to his government all which may concern it and to affect the course of events, so far as he is able to do so, in favor of his own country. No one has understood or performed these duties in Washington, within my experience, better than William Herridge. I am not concerned here with what he did—so long ago—but with how he did it.

As the New Deal began its improvisations, Canada was deeply concerned with the effect upon its economy of the controls exercised over agriculture by the Agricultural Adjustment Administration, over manufacture and commerce by the National Industrial Recovery Administration, and over the gold value of the dollar by the United States Treasury and the Reconstruction Finance Corporation. While government management of the economy was decreed from the highest quarters, the incidence of the controls was guided importantly by the able young academicians and lawyers brought into the new bureaucracy of the multifarious alphabetical agencies. Access to cabinet officers is easy for a diplomat of Herridge's ability and charm. His special achievement was to establish easy and friendly relations with the bureaucracy. His methods were so simple and intelligent in their understanding of his problem as to be unique.

The first was the luncheon for men. Herridge did not deprecate the contribution of women to diplomatic method, but this required, so he thought, the more leisurely dinner and evening conversation. His luncheons were small, six or eight; his guests, of little-cabinet rank, and never more than one from the same department or agency. He sat down promptly at 1:00, not waiting for later arrivals, and ended the lunch as promptly at 2:00. There were no cocktails, but an excellent white wine with the meal, which, in turn, was light, well chosen, well cooked, and served with flair by Horsely, the butler—as much of a character as the Minister.

Herridge's part was to stimulate conversation. At this he was a past master. He would poke fun at himself, in a delightfully slow, clowning manner, for his inability to grasp the current crop of rumors and leaks, and make such gay nonsense of them, and of the rivalries between the cabinet prima donnas, that his guests would take over the talk and vie with one another to make all clear. Dawning understanding from Herridge and wholly erroneous guesses as to the future would bring forth further enlightenment. Sometimes he would speak hopelessly of some predicament which Canadian interests faced, often stimulating helpful suggestions.

His guests would leave in good time, having had a delightful hour, pleased with their own performances and without a trace of the heavy somnolence which usually follows a diplomatic luncheon.

Another occasion which much tempted Herridge was the departmental or agency outing, more common in the days when everything was smaller in this city. The Canadian Minister was a sought-after guest. He was particularly successful as a soft-ball relief pitcher for the civil servants against the political officers. Today, I suppose, he would be said to be "projecting an image in depth." But in those days he was getting to know more people, picking up more information, and dropping seeds in friendly minds.

During his stay with us there were few members of the administration who knew as much about what was going on as Herridge; and there were none who were as reticent in talking about it as he. When he went home to attempt the role of a political power behind the scenes—a role which proved a sad disappointment for him—for many of us much of the sparkle went out of our lives. I, for one, who for a treasured time used to walk with him every afternoon, knew that something irreplaceable had gone. We have already missed him for a long time.

Part Seven ≪≪

What Goes into Love of Country

The Land in American Life

The feelings which I have at being with you here this evening spring from the roots of my life. Here my parents came to live and work among you nearly sixty years ago. Into this community and this church they have poured two lives of ceaseless devotion. Here my brother and sister and I were born, and spent our youth, in that quiet past which now seems another world. Out of this soil I grew. It has entered into me and is a part of me as I am of it.

This bond between a man and the early surroundings which molded and shaped him is not only the strongest of ties; it is one which becomes more important than ever to us in this age when human problems on a wider scale have become so vast and so

Made on the occasion of the 200th anniversary of the Holy Trinity Parish at Middletown, Conn., on Apr. 17, 1950, *Department of State Bulletin,* Vol. XXIV, May 1, 1950.

baffling. The first youthful knowledge of human relationships, in which the path of duty was recogniz-
able and in which moral values were plain, is for many
of us one of the few fixed points in the turmoil and
confusion of the world today.

Without these fixed points, we would have nothing
to hold onto. If these familiar objects and values which
surround us here, and which give to this place its
character, are not real, then nothing is real. If they
are not valid, then there is no validity in the assump-
tions of our national life. Those of us whose fate it is
to occupy ourselves with national affairs may apply
ourselves as we like in that whirlpool of activity, but
make no mistake about it: it is this source—the neighborhood and the community, as we knew them and
recollect them—to which we must return for the inspiration and the faith to sustain our effort. Without
it there is no substance in what we do.

We in this parish have heard many times the words,
"In my Father's house are many mansions." In this
country of ours, there are many hometowns. They
are not all alike in their traditions and outlook. It is
not necessary that they should be. The glory of our
country lies in its ability to accept and reconcile diversity. Local differences in origin are not clashing
elements. They are complementary and mutually
sustaining in a way that is possible only in a free
society. For that reason, one American's pride in his
home environment is a thing that every other American understands and approves, whether or not that
environment is his own. And behind all the good-

238

natured rivalry and boasting which we like to attach to our local origin, is the recognition that the experience of growing up in any American community, from Connecticut to California, constitutes the indelible stamp of nationality. This is why when from one American impulse or another we move to other areas, other States, we find ourselves at ease and at home. This is what makes us Americans.

There are few communities that can look back on a longer and deeper participation in the molding of the national tradition than Middletown. This parish is two hundred years old today. But the community in which it is centered predates it by exactly a century. In the fall of this year you will be celebrating its three hundredth anniversary. Our fellow townsman and distinguished American historian, John Fiske, described it in 1900 as "the very central home and nursing place of the ideas and institutions which today constitute the chief greatness of America." These are deep roots and impressive ones.

It is not strange that this was so. Life in the Connecticut Valley three centuries ago bred strong and self-reliant men and women. The Valley was the gateway to the West which meant western Massachusetts —to the frontier at Springfield and Deerfield with all its dangers—to the land beyond in Vermont and New Hampshire. Eleazor Wheelock went up the Valley from New Haven to teach the Indians at Hanover. The route to this new country followed the great river. There were many stout hearts to take it.

As the years moved on, men of the Valley began to

look down the river and beyond the Sound and the ocean to China. Ships began to sail to the Far East and back again, up the river, with silk, tea, and furs. Many of you can remember the customs house which still stood on Main Street when I was a boy. And the old houses on High Street bear witness that the adventurous spirits who sailed these ships were good traders.

All of this, as I have said, bred strong characters. And not only strong characters but opinionated and contentious ones. These were no men—or women either—to take their opinions and beliefs ready-made from anyone else. An early order of the General Court of Connecticut, referring to the citizens of Middletown, took special note of what it called "the unsuitableness in their spirits."

So it was not always easy for them to agree among themselves, any more than it is for us today. Issues were vigorously and stubbornly contested. But it was characteristic of them that in the end they always found some practical settlement.

At the two hundred and fiftieth anniversary celebration of the town, in 1900, the Reverend Frederick Green, then pastor of the South Congregational Church, told of the dispute over the location of the Third Meeting House. "There was so much danger of friction," he said, "between those living on what they called the west and north and east sides of the square bounded by Main and High Streets, that it was decided to leave the question of the site to the Lord's decision by means of the lot. And the lot having fallen upon the south corner, where no one desired it, they bowed to the Lord's will and built at the head of Church Street."

Tolerance, in particular, did not come easily or quickly to these early settlers. When this parish was founded on that Easter Monday, in 1750, it was not easy for its members even to get a permit to build an Anglican church in the community. On the third try, they were given the swampiest spot in town, where many of the city fathers thought no church could be built. Yet persistence and determination seem, as so often in American life, to have triumphed without bitterness. We are told that when the problems of terrain had been conquered the completion of the frame of the first church building was marked by a cheer which could be heard a mile away.

The qualities which make possible a free life in a free country—self-reliance, self-respect, and respect for the rights and opinions of others—were obviously not brought here as a finished product by the early settlers. They had to be built up slowly, beginning with the very foundations, like that first church building— despite the unfirm, and at first glance, unpromising terrain of human recalcitrance which had to underlie them. They were forged in the great and unique experience of American national life. They are still being forged there today. And perhaps the greatest task of our time is to see that all this, which it took so many generations to create, is not lost in a single generation—that, on the contrary, we continue to add our own contributions to this edifice of freedom which

What Goes into Love of Country

will never be entirely finished and which is being so
sorely tested today.

It is fashionable nowadays to interpret the state of
mind of the American people to explain what they
are like, what they are thinking, what they intend.
Perhaps, because I was born and bred in New England, I am inclined to be skeptical of such preten-
sions. In New England, we don't think of the American people as a vast human herd having herd opinions
which can be summed up in a sentence or a slogan.
We think of them rather as individuals having, each
of them, an opinion of his own. We regard it indeed
as the distinguishing characteristic of American society
that men here are individuals who make up their individual minds and think and speak as they please,
answerable only to their consciences and their God.
That distinguishing American characteristic is, as we
see it, the contribution of those founders of these
states who built their houses in the wilderness because freedom of mind and freedom of conscience
were worth more to them than all the rest together.

But it is not only because New Englanders bred the
passion for individual freedom into the American bone
that we respect men who think for themselves, we
respect them also because we have learned by long
experience that men who make up their minds for
themselves are stronger than other men and more reliable in time of trouble. We like that quality in a
man. We even like it in a neighbor whose opinions
differ from our own and who holds to them, as New
England neighbors sometimes do, with what seems to

us on occasions like obstinate stubbornness. We respect a man who knows what he thinks because it is he—not someone else—who thinks it. And we have confidence in a country in which men like that still live.

It is for that reason, I think, that we New Englanders, dour and skeptical as we are thought to be, believe so profoundly in this country and its future. We may have our reservations about one administration or another, and we may believe that this party or that is taking us down the road to ruin, but we never doubt in our hearts that the fundamental strength of the American people, the strength of a nation of individuals in which men think and speak for themselves, will surmount all difficulties. And as to that, in my opinion, we are right.

This thought has peculiar force here in the Connecticut River Valley by virtue of the changes which have taken place over these three hundred years. The descendants of those early settlers constitute today only one element of the inhabitants of the Valley. They have been steadily joined by new arrivals. Those new arrivals had different backgrounds, different religions, different political origins. They were from Ireland and Poland. They were Italians, Germans, and Swedes and may I add at least one Canadian. In 1940, almost 20 percent of the people in the state were foreign-born.

My own parents, like those of many of you here tonight, belonged to that 20 percent of your people who had come here from other countries. Yet so strong was the yeast of Connecticut life that it leavened the whole and in almost no time at all the newcomers were New Englanders to the core—making their own way, shouldering responsibilities, strongly holding and expressing their own opinions.

One of my earliest memories is of walking with my father, the first thing in the morning, from the house on Broad Street to the post office. We would go down the boardwalk behind the house, past the church, and then along the block on Main Street to the old brownstone building. It was not all joy. For the second store on Main Street was Mr. Walsh's harness store. He would be standing in the doorway beside the great wooden horse, which in some way I thought was the one Ulysses had made. Mr. Walsh seemed to me Jovelike, with his gray beard covering the top of his working apron, and infinitely old—although I imagine that he was younger than I am now.

Then would begin what was a combination of the 8 o'clock news of the world today, a Capitol Cloakroom, and Town Meeting of the Air. Customers and passers-by joined in. Every subject was taken to pieces, sometimes put together again, and sometimes just left lying around—wars, politics, the Irish question, the tariff question, Queen Victoria's Diamond Jubilee, and the sad propensity of mankind for strong liquors and the best method for the control thereof. Everyone had strong opinions on nearly all subjects, and some apparently believed that all facts were created free and equal.

My legs would begin to ache, and my spirits sag with them. To pull at my father's coat involved hazards not to be lightly risked, and I would end up sitting sadly on the platform of the wooden horse. Fast time for those two blocks from the house to the post office was an hour. But it was making New Englanders of all of us.

It was making more than New Englanders, in fact: It was making Americans. For in the life of this place, and of many others like it, there was embodied something which has always seemed to me to be the essence of Americanism—the recognition of individuality as the foundation of human society, the respect by the groups for the human individual, regardless of his origin or his station in life, and as a *quid pro quo* for that respect, the acknowledgment by the individual of his share of responsibility for his own fortunes and for the fortunes of the community.

Through the operation of these qualities, the foundations of society have come to rest in America on the voluntary participation of the individual in the activity of the group, with the recognition that the structure will stand or fall with the quality of his participation. It is these things: this recognition of the individual dignity by the community and this recognition of his own responsibility by the individual, that stand out to me as the essential characteristics of this community in which I grew up and which, to my mind, give meaning and purpose to the great struggles of national policy in which our people are now engaged.

The connection between these two things is intimate and unbreakable. The quality of American patriotism—the quality of the American's attitude toward his national community—is not only linked with the relationship of the individual to the community in which he resides: it stems from that relation, it draws its strength from it. And it is this which gives us the conviction of the justice and the terrible urgency of our national cause.

It is our glory and our pride that our attitude toward our country springs from our individual experiences, from the impressions of our childhood, from the moral convictions which we picked up on these streets and in these schools and churches, and not from an imposed political doctrine. This gives us a strength in our national purposes which is rarely revealed on the surface of our public life except in times of national crisis. There are other parts of the world where the centralized power of the state is an impressive crust, concealing a vast pulp of human misery and helplessness. We spurn that type of impressiveness. We rejoice in the fact that the real elements of our immense strength are present here, where they are perhaps least conspicuous: at the foundations of our society, in the homes and the shaded streets of many tens of thousands of quiet and decent and God-fearing American communities.

It is this thought that carries many of us now, as it has carried many of our predecessors, through moments which, without it, might shake the strongest faith and the strongest resolve. It is this thought which gives us calmness and strength of spirit amid the tumult and the shouting, like a glimpse of the stars through a break in the clouds.

246

The Bible in Our National Life

Today we inaugurate a new version, a new translation of the Bible. It is right and necessary that these eternal and vigorously living books should continually be reborn in fresh and living words, just as the earth is continuously reborn and renewed. It is right, too, that many of us should cling to the older words—particularly those who, if they apply Lincoln's phrase to themselves, must describe themselves as old men. For when he said that of himself in February, 1861, he was almost ten years younger than I am now.

We are made from the soil out of which we grew. And as we grow older we continually go back to origins. For each of us those origins are different.

Made before a meeting sponsored jointly by the National Council of Churches of Christ in the U.S.A. and the Washington Federation of Churches at the National Guard Armory, Washington, D.C., on Sept. 29, 1952. *Department of State Bulletin,* Vol. XXVII, October 13, 1952.

What Goes into Love of Country

For me they lie in the Connecticut Valley and in the King James Version As my mind goes back beyond clear memory, there is a merging. Soon we shall come to All Saints' Day and the Advent season. The mail trucks will exhort us to mail Christmas packages early and tell us the days that remain. This brings to me, like wood smoke, memories not seen but felt— the squeak of dry snow under foot, voices no longer heard, the laughter of greetings about a doorway, the steam of breath in the cold air and these words:

> And it came to pass in those days, that there went out a decree from Caesar Augustus that all the world should be taxed. And this taxing was first made when Cyrenius was governor of Syria. And all went to be taxed, every one unto his own city.

Then one knew that it was indeed Christmas.

So our rejoicing in a new version of the Bible does not, and need not, diminish our love for the older ones.

Apart from the familiarity with a particular version which engages our affections, the important thing for us is the place of these books in the civilization which we have inherited and which we are strengthening and defending in our own lives and in the national life of our country.

Its place is enormous—shared only, I think, by the influence of the land itself, the country in which we live. I am not forgetful of the great inheritance of Greek thought—indeed it is felt in these books themselves—or Roman institutions, or of the effect of the ideas and passions which spread across the ocean from eighteenth-century France and England. But the effect of this Bible and this country were in my judgment predominant. And effect upon what? And this forms the third element to produce the United States of America—the people who came here and who were born here.

In the earliest days in the Northeast, the Book was All. The settlers came here to live their own reading of it. It was the spiritual guide, the moral and legal code, the political system, the sustenance of life, whether that meant endurance of hardship, the endless struggle with nature, battle with enemies, or the inevitable processes of life and death. And it meant to those who cast the mold of this country something very specific and very clear. It meant that the purpose of man's journey through this life was to learn and identify his life and effort with the purpose and the will of God. To do this he must purge his nature of its rebellious side. And this, in turn, meant that the struggle between good and evil was the raging, omnipresent battle in every life, every day.

The test was not one's own will or desire, not the dictate of the government, not the opinion of the day, but the will of God as revealed by the prophets and to be found, in the last analysis, by the individual conscience—guided, instructed, chastened, but in the end, alone.

Out of the travail of these lives the idea of God-fearing was given powerful content and effect. It meant a voluntary, eager, even militant submission to a moral order overriding the wills of the low and

What Goes into Love of Country

great and of the state itself. And this carried with it the notion of restraints against all, of areas blocked off into which none might enter because here the duty of the individual conscience must be performed.

But this was not all. This did not exhaust the teachings of this Bible. For it taught also that the fear of God was the love of God and that the love of God was the love of man and the service of man.

What was written in the Book was taught also by the life of this country. Never was self-reliance so linked with mutual help as in those early days, when from birth to death neighbor turned to neighbor for help and received it in overflowing measure. No characteristic so marks Americans to this day as this quick and helping hand, a hand offered not only to our fellow citizens but to our fellowmen.

It shocks and surprises us to be told that this is a weak and soft attitude. A few weeks ago I read to another audience the teaching which is being given to a people who only a few years ago regarded us as friends. Here it is:

> Soviet patriotism is indissolubly connected with hatred toward the enemies of the Socialist Fatherland. "It is impossible to conquer the enemy without having learned to hate him with all the might of one's soul. . . ." The teaching of hatred toward the enemies of the toilers enriches the conception of Socialistic humanism by distinguishing it from sugary and hypocritical "philanthropy."

This is a quotation from a Soviet encyclopedia.

Now philanthropy means love of man. It is sad and

tragic that a people who once read the same books should be taught today to hate in order to avoid the softness of the love of man.

In order to love our own country we do not have to hate anyone. There is enough to inspire love here. And the first thing is the country itself. I am not speaking now of abstractions, the national entity, its institutions, its history, and power—great as these are— but of some piece of earth with the sky over it, whoever owns it, which we think of when we think of our country. For it is this love of a specific place which gives great strength and comfort to the human heart.

Not far from here there are a few acres which even to think of brings me peace, and to be on, to see and touch, gives unending joy and refreshment. They came to me from the same family which received them from the Lord Proprietor and which, at the beginning of our country's history, built a modest house under the trees. Here for generations men and women have worked hard and with loving care to make a livelihood and to make a home. The house, the barn, the workshop were built to outlast the centuries and have done so. To every effort nature has responded a thousandfold, entering a partnership to make the land each season more beautiful than before—the turf softer and richer, the trees greater to shelter the small house under their embracing spread. To carry on man's side of this partnership brings a sense of merging with the land and with the generations who have been at one with it before.

It is a good beginning to the love of country to

love some small piece of it very much.

And, finally, the central figure of this heritage—man himself. Who are these people, the Americans? They are a people who, as we have said, hold sacred the Word of God. They are a people molded by the dangers and the beauty and the open bounty of this continent.

Out of many, they are one. Theirs is a unity based upon the brotherhood of man under the Fatherhood of God; theirs, too, the great and vigorous diversity based on respect for man, the individual. Here is no orthodoxy, no worship of authority. At the center of this society stands the individual man. His back is straight, he looks you in the eye—and calls no man his master. Sometimes our friends abroad ask whether, because of our machines and our worries about the world, we are losing this American quality, whether a pressure for uniformity is gradually turning us into so many sausages, all alike, in our dress, our thinking and in the way we live. I do not think this will be our fate. We are too proud, too stubborn, too cussedly independent for the bridle. And this, indeed, is the secret of our strength, and of the lasting power of our society. For the solidarity which is built, not upon servility, but upon the common loyalty of free men, is resilient and enduring.

And the source and record of the spiritual purpose of this community of men is the Holy Writ—the Book which brings us together this evening. This occasion reminds us of the tremendous vitality of these writings, which form the core, the vertebra of our society.

The Bible in Our National Life

These reflections upon the interplay of the Bible, the land, and the people in creating the national life of our country are made vivid for me as I go home these autumn evenings. With me, as I leave, are the worries, the exasperations, the frustrations of the day. Then the rush of the city traffic falls away. Instead there are fields and lines of cattle facing the same way, with heads down. Lights spring up in the thinning houses. In time, the road becomes a dirt lane, which leads through a grove of oaks around a Quaker Meeting House, hidden in its ivy, beside it, the graveyard, with its rows of little headstones. I know that as I breast the hill, there will be lights at the end of the lane.

And there is peace.

And I think of the moving prayer that we should be kept all the day long of this troublous life 'til the shadows lengthen, and the evening comes, and the busy world is hushed and the fever of life is over; and our work is done; and that then we be given a safe lodging and a holy rest and peace at the last.

In the times in which we live there is no safe lodging and no rest. But all that we do and shall do is that there may be peace among men. So striving, we may find peace within ourselves.

DATE DUE

GAYLORD			PRINTED IN U.S.A.